LIFE IN THE AIR

TRUE STORIES OF ADVENTURE AND
MISADVENTURE ALOFT

C. S. Pascarell

Copyright © 2022 by C. S. Pascarell/DM Universal Inc.

All rights reserved. No part of this book may be reproduced or transmitted in any form or by any means without written permission from the author.

Paperback ISBN: 978-1-963250-47-3

For Carrie

Contents

ACKNOWLEDGEMENT 1

FOREWORD 2

INTRODUCTION 4

FIRST FLIGHT FRIGHT 5

NIGHT SHOT 16

A NIGHT ON THE PLATFORM (PART 1) 26

A NIGHT ON THE PLATFORM (PART 2) 41

YOYO TANKER 57

COMPLICATIONS 74

VERTIGO 87

THE MYSTERIOUS ISLAND 94

NIKKI'S FLIGHT 98

FULTON 107

THE REDHAWKS: FROM THE COCKPIT 115

HARRY 122

THE FLYBY 128

TERMINAL VELOCITY 132

THE PARISIAN ADVENTURE 144

THE GREATEST FLYER OF THEM ALL! 165

GLOSSARY 170

ABOUT THE AUTHOR 173

ACKNOWLEDGEMENT

I've spent the better part of my life in pursuit of all the excitement flying has to offer. I was singularly focused, with a passion and drive that, some would say, bordered on obsession. And though that measure of ambition can be beneficial… without *opportunity*, I'd just be another hapless dreamer. Fortunately, and chiefly due to the opportunities provided me by a handful of caring individuals, my life in the air was as rewarding and colorful as any flier could hope for.

I am particularly indebted to Budd Davisson who was predominantly responsible for much of my exotic airplane adventures and experience. He, along with Jim Moser and Harry Shepard were responsible, in large part, for my development as an aviator and, for that, and to them I am eternally grateful.

Thanks also to Lou Drendel, for much of the illustrations contained herein.

I also would like to extend a special thank you to Mr. Dean McInnis, whose encouragement and logistical support were instrumental in bringing this book to fruition.

It is indeed unfortunate that I can't personally acknowledge all the people who played a part in my aeronautical development. So, to my many colleagues, team mates and friends, with whom I shared a love for aviation, and from whom I learned, was inspired, and towards whom I felt a special kinship… Thank You All.

FOREWORD

The task at hand is to write a profound foreword for the unique writings of one of the most unique individuals most of us have ever met. Unique in a good way… and I don't have a clue where or how to start. This from a guy who routinely authors something like 250,000 words a year and I can't put together a thousand measly words about one of my best and most impressive friends? Shame on me!

I don't know how many of the world's top pilots have used him as the measuring stick when describing how good someone is. At the same time, I'm positive not one of those who have trusted their lives to his flying skills have read a single word of his prose. This is because he has made no effort to make it known that many of us who wordsmith for a living absolutely admire his ability with the written word. It matches his ability with an airplane, and his understanding of and his connection with the human condition. Frankly, I for one, am jealous of his ability to paint a picture of life in the air - Of so many different lives in the air. It might be the instantaneous deciding of a course of action when an airplane unexpectedly decides to quit flying. Or maybe while flying upside down and sliding into tight formation, separated by only a foot or two. With this minimum separation they do loops and rolls in the canopy to canopy "mirror" position. I don't know which is the most impressive – The ability to do something like that or the ability to tell the rest of the world how it is done, and how it feels.

Aviation, in all its widely disparate variations involves all our senses. Our sight, our smell, our emotions. The way it can make our minds think we are doing something we're not. The way it can take us places where very few have been. Be it the adrenalin fueled launch off a dark flight deck on tip of a 42,000-pound Roman Candle, or the feeling of taxiing up in front of a cheering air show crowd and have a nine-year-old enthusiast ask for your autograph.

It's one thing to experience something, it is entirely something different to be capable of painting the proper emotional and mental image with words so that the experience is shared by others on a visceral level. Carl does that in these pages. The words have been a lifetime coming and they have an attraction that reaches outside of the cockpit to the hearts and souls of those who appreciate a tale well told. And a flier's life well lived. Well done Carl Pascarell!! It's about time!

Budd Davisson 2023

INTRODUCTION

Dear Reader

I titled this book "Life in the Air" and significantly *not* "My ~~Life~~ in the Air" because, although these are my experiences, my recollections, my wish is to share with you the unique way in which some of these very human experiences become an intimate part of one's being: experiences that excite a person, that move a person, and ultimately, change a person. Things that are not unique to me, the person, but exist as true wonders of life at which *anyone* would marvel. Wonders, without which life would seem far less colorful.

I challenge you to come away unmoved.

Imagine:

- The shear majesty of a seventy-thousand-foot, internally lit, towering cumulonimbus storm boiling up through a full moonlit overcast somewhere over the Mid Atlantic
- That first glimpse of the earth's curvature from 55,000 feet.
- Those ink-black, pitching deck nights at the ship with no divert options.
- That moment of pride when you see in your student's eyes that they finally "get it".
- The spark lit in your young passenger on their first flight that launches them into a lifetime of adventures in the air.

These things can make a difference in a person…in *any* person.

These and others are out there still… And they are yours for the taking… Happy Hunting !

FIRST FLIGHT FRIGHT

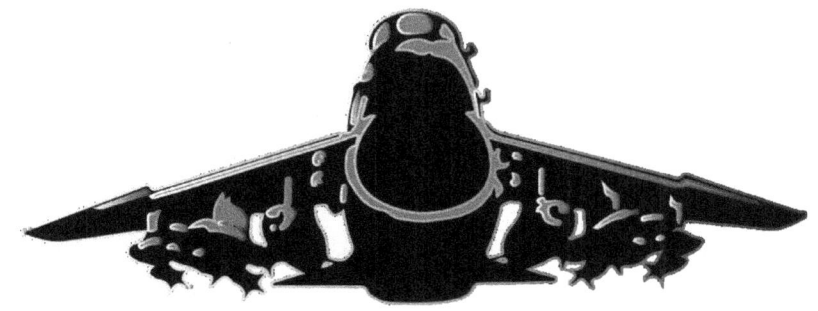

Early morning, late October, many years ago, a much younger me, laden with all the fighter pilot accouterments, sauntered up to the 36,000-pound, fire-breathing monster sitting innocently on the tarmac at the Naval Air Station, Cecil Field, Florida, waiting patiently for its latest, unsuspecting victim.

Next to me on the flight line, preflighting his own jet, is Lt. Terry Miller, my chase pilot and instructor for this, my maiden hop in the Vought A7E Corsair II.

I hang my helmet bag on the retractable steps to the cockpit of the aircraft just as the plane captain comes backing out of the intake, having just completed his "duct diving" FOD check ritual.

"Looks good, sir".

"Thanks, Wilson"

My subsequent preflight reveals a sea-weary, battle-tested brute dripping with the ever-present hydraulic leaks that every experienced A-7 driver has come to expect and, in turn, disregard. Accordingly, I acquiesce to their more seasoned judgment, overlook the red puddles collecting on the concrete, and hasten up and into the cockpit, ready and eager to get going.

Settling into the cockpit, I strap in, plug in and begin the tedious process of checks and set-ups -- Initializing, testing, twisting and turning. No surprises, everyday systems stuff, but time-consuming, still. The airplane, I note, very definitely lacks the simplicity of the A4, my previous mount.

I move slowly through it all, just like the "sim", careful not to miss anything, and when done, I still have three minutes to go on the Inertial Systems alignment. Next door, Terry's all ready to go, waiting patiently... drumming his fingers on the canopy rail...no rush... ho hum... bored, I'm sure, with the whole thing....

The Inertial system is finally ready—time to go. Mask on, canopy closed, deep breath...ready to start. What next...what next... looking around the cockpit... What am I forgetting...hmm...I guess I'm ready... I look outside. There's plane captain Wilson, hands on hips... I can just hear him thinking, "damn rookies", suddenly even more unhappy with his Saturday morning shift.

OK...OK... let's crank it—two-finger spin-up signal. Engine turns... igniters... .and throttle to idle... click... whir... thud ... whoosh, and we're up and running. N1's at idle. TOT within limits. Disconnect external air...engine oil temp, and pressure looks good... So, again to Wilson... Run through the pantomimed control checks and flap setting with him out front, a quick com check with Terry, and we're ready to taxi. The marshaller directs us out of the flight line and kicks me onto the north-south taxiway. A quick salute to him, and we're on our way. Just that quick.

Thumbing the mic, I call for taxi, a flight of two, and we slowly make our way to the runway's end - me trying hard to think of anything I may have missed and Terry following obediently along

LIFE IN THE AIR

100 feet in trail, no doubt, wondering why he's even flying on a Saturday.

At the end of the runway and holding short, I run through my takeoff checks and triple-check the *really* important things—ejection seat armed, flaps set, and wings spread and locked. I review in my mind the SID, com plan, and abort procedure. Nothing left to do, all is in order...I guess I'm ready...time to go.

So, I switch to the tower, take a quick check over my shoulder, get the thumbs up from Terry, and we are set, mask on.

"Cecil Tower, Razor 24 and flight, holding short, ready to go".

"Razor 24, flight of two, switch to departure, runway 36 left, cleared for takeoff".

Quick last check now, radios over to departure, canopy locked, shoulder harness locked, flaps set.

On the runway now. I hold the brakes... the power comes up—80 percent, gauges all good, N1, N2, TOP... control check.. hydraulics steady, Mil power.. brakes released, and I'm off!

Good accel... Off the nose gear steering. directional control good....

80 knots...quick scan inside... engine's good...no lights...

Faster and faster...110...120... 130, time to fly. nice and easy now... easy rotation... nose comes up and the airplane smoothly slides into the air... nice. just as sweet as can be...100 feet... gear up... 200 feet...flaps u.....

WAAHHBAAANG!!!!   MASSIVE   VIBRATION!!

DECELLING RAPIDLY!!! COCKPIT SHAKING!!!

EVERYTHING'S A BLUR!!! WHAT THE...??

Helmet rattles my head!! WARNING LIGHTS ARE lit up all over the cockpit!! What the Fu...!!! THINK!! STAY WITH IT!!! Trying to hang on...SETTLING!! Settling!
OH, fuuu....150 feet! ...
GOING DOWN!!!
AIRSPEED'S FALLING FAST!!! GONNA STALL!!! FLAPS DOWN!!!, GET 'EM DOWN!! QUICK!!
GET THE FLAPS OUT!!!
I slam the flap lever to full down.... **EYES FIGHTING TO FOCUS!!... THE LEADING EDGE IS OUT...** Trailing edge slowly coming....
WE'RE STILL COMING DOWN!!! AIRPLANE MUSHING TOWARD THE TREES...
NOSE COMES UP...
Rudder shaker stall warning kicks in, nonstop against my feet, screaming for attention!
EASY WITH IT!!
DON'T STALL IT!!
In my blurred periphery, I catch Terry zinging by on my right... his gear and flaps coming back out, backpedaling, trying to stay with me...wondering, I'm sure, WTF!! Warning annunciators lit up all over the place, flashing hysterically for attention but unreadable in the Cuisinart in which I suddenly find myself.....THINKING EJECT..THINKING REAL HARD, REAL FAST..NOT NOW... RIGHT SMACK ON

TOP OF THE weapons storage facility... not a good idea...stay with it... the angle of attack way high, rudder shaker desperately pounding at my feet, adding to the cacophonous tumult ...100

feet...and settling, slowly...

Terry's distorted yells break through the tempest of my sensory overload ...

"CLIMB! CLIMB! CLIMB !!!!" me: "UNNNAABBLE!!"

... 75 feet ... THROTTLE BENT FORWARD, still on the shaker... 50 feet...tall trees go whizzing by...I am THINKING REAL HARD ABOUT THE EJECTION HANDLE...50 feet...

ENGINES COMING APART...SHIT !!...telephone poles whiz by... I can touch them!... 50 feet....50 feet...and holding... holding...barely... but holding... 50 feet...angle of attack dangerously high...Stall warning relentless   Mushing across the landscape. Terry's close enough now to see what's going on: the tremulous blur of a pilot only half in control of an airplane that's quickly coming apart around him.

Terry: "HIT YOUR DUMPS!! DUMPS!!! DUMPS!!"

SHIT! I should have thought of that.

I mash the dump switch to help lighten the load... Compressor section air pressurizes the wing tanks, and fuel starts

pouring out of the wing dump nozzles, swirling gigantic liquid spirals, majestic in the super high lift vortex. Any other time it'd be a beautiful display of mixed fluid technologies, but right now, I'm not at all impressed. I need to get rid of several thousand pounds of dead weight dragging me down... keeping me from turning, climbing and flying. The beauty of the scene will have to wait... I only wish I had stores on the wing I could "pickle" off...Heading straight out over the trees... looking for wires, towers...a way out...a way back....no turning... barely holding on to the air... Eject? Eject? The question won't leave me alone, waiting for an answer I'm not yet ready to give. The vibration suddenly eases or maybe I'm getting used to it. I'm finally able to read warnings... annunciator flashing "ENGINE HOT" ...no shit...

"oil pressure low" and several other things I can't at all make out, or don't want to.

Terry finally reconfigured and dropped back just off my right wing... dumping fuel and "S" turning to keep from overrunning me... Again... it must be a hell of a sight, a pair of pair of A7s at treetop level, flames shooting out the ass end of one, and both dumping fuel all over North Florida.

Terry, "Try and get it turned around!!" Me, my voice, staccato with airframe vibration, "Caaannntt!

Bbaaarrrelllyy....Ffllyiiinggg"

Even still, three miles north of the field, I've got to do something to get this thing turned around before it quits for good or I run into something. Fuel dump is taking hold, AOA is coming down...but it is still on the ragged edge... I don't know how much longer things will hold together... Gotta get it turned around, I've got to try...

Me: "commiiinng leefft"

I gingerly start a 5-degree bank turn left. It feels like I'm dragging my wingtip through the trees... After 90 degrees of turn, I look back over my shoulder and see a mile-long swath of jet fuel settling, still wet, into the trees... EPA's gonna love that. I continue my turn...BIG turn... easy turn... Nice and smooth... roll out now...heading south... Over the golf course...duffers gawking awestruck at the impending disaster unfolding over their heads...downwind, or something like that...Wings level again... I'm finally able to climb, if you can call it that...barely...slowly, too slowly. I claw my way up to 100 feet...every foot a battle... every knot, a tiny treasure.   even a hundred feels, all of a sudden, like a thousand, compared to where I was, but I still can't see the field.   and a hundred is all she's gonna go...

Terry to the rescue, "Field's 10 o'clock, 6 miles, hang in there, I'll call your turn."

"rrojjjj"

100 feet, the field is abeam 5 miles or so. The AOA's improving...still way beyond optimum... Way behind the power curve, plowing through the air, grotesquely nose high, more drag than lift...aircraft stubbornly refuses to accelerate... to fly... to behave.... And I still have to get the gear out. It seems like every light on the panel and side console is lit up or flashing. Annoying... screaming for attention when I've got none left over to give... I know! ...I know!!! Nothing I can do about any of them right now anyway.... I just have to get it on the ground...FAST!! I angle in towards the field... 150 feet now... scanning the horizon... The first thing I spot is the Control Tower, poking up above the pines.... Heading generally in the right direction...turbulence rocks at me, and I'm suddenly back down to 50 feet... crap!

Terry, "Start your turn in."

Me, "Hold on...I gotta get it stable."

Then... Got it... field in sight... FIELD IN SIGHT!!.... Keep the turn coming... keep it commin... don't want to overshoot...

Terry: "Hook down."

I throw the hook out without a thought. He wants me to trap, I'll trap...No argument there...no time to even think about it... I just want to get it on the ground...I just want to hit concrete... barely able level flight... gonna have to wait till the very end for the gear...turn has us intercepting the centerline a mile out.... Way low... Glideslope meatball off the bottom... me trying to gather a couple more knots before I throw the gear out... Half a mile...Come on, baby... keep runnin...just a few seconds more...come on...Engine starts making a funny high pitch grinding noise...eating itself...louder and louder...its thrust comes in pulses...the dying heart's last beats the next beat could be its last...

Terry, "Kill your dumps."

SHIT again! Mash the dumps to off...quarter mile now... I've got the runway made ...I think...not sure the gear is gonna have time to fully extend... Whatever... I'm landing. Crossing the threshold at 50 feet, GEAR NOW! big clunk ...slowly the gear falls into place... one green, 25 feet, ...airspeed falling fast!... come on...come on... Hold it off! Hold it off! ...and... three green!!! Touchdown!! On centerline... 300 feet before the gear...keep it there... keep it there... arresting gear coming up... hang on!... GGRAAAH!!! My hook snags the wire, and I slam forward under the deceleration... damn!... shit! Dragged to a stop...stopped...shut it down...shut it down!!! Shut it down and breathe...and just that quick, it's over...I sit frozen in shocked thought while the silent stillness engulfs me....

Shaking, I unclench my hands from their death grip on the stick and throttle as the engine whines its slow, broken metal death. Damn...and damn..Heart pounding...breathe...breathe...heart pounding...my inner self screaming "quit daydreaming and get out!!! Get out !!!" Snapping back to reality, I unstrap and jump down out of the cockpit, scrambling clumsily to get away from anything that might be thinking about blowing up.

Crash crew, lights flashing, sirens screaming screeches to a halt alongside, all silver suited and ready for action. Hoses come out, and cooling fog showers the airplane. Steam hisses, boiling off the sides of the fuselage. I stare, gaping stupidly at the scene before me, for a full 30 seconds before common sense takes over, and I head for cover. I scurry over to stand with some of the crash guys, safe behind their largest truck, just happy to be alive and breathing, and giddy all of a sudden with a copious adrenaline rush.

"Sheez, you guys are quick," I offer...

The crustiest of the silver men, "Never seen a Corsair with afterburner... figured you'd be back soon enough."

Me, "Yea, well, I was beginning to think I might just be walking back...thanks just the same for being here."

Him, "S'what we do..."

Post-flight inspection finds the paint almost gone, completely blistered along the aft fuselage. Even after 15 minutes, from 3 feet away, and despite the crash crew's earlier cooling shower, I can still feel the heat emanating from the side of the airplane. The engine was toast, melted down and broken up...dead.

I ride with the crash guys back to the Squadron's maintenance office, overwhelmed with relief when exhaustion hits me like a lead pipe. Slogging into the Maintenance Office, I fill out the discrepancy log, dump my gear in the paraloft and drive home in a near-crippling daze of conflicting emotions and physical exhaustion. First flight, indeed...

Subsequent engine teardown revealed a failed inlet guide vane to be the culprit. After that initial failure and because of

some funky airflow in the compressor section, the busted guide vane actually got sucked forward through the engine, taking out several stages of compressor blades before the whole bunch turned around and blasted its way aft, gutting the core compressor and turbine sections before blowing itself out the tailpipe white hot. The Vought engineers estimated that only the fan air from the Corsair's high bypass fanjet was left available for thrust, and it was that alone that kept me in the air. Well... that and plenty of luck, I don't mind admitting.

For me, that first flight was a profoundly eye-opening experience. A trial-by-fire introduction to the nasty side of one airplane's personality, an airplane with whom I'd be destined to spend the next three years or so, flying missions far more trying in environs not nearly so benevolent as todays. I had much to look forward to... much to learn... much to survive.

In retrospect, and to be completely honest about it, if I had known what I know now, I'd have probably jumped out of the airplane right away. But to me, at that time, I didn't have a really good idea of just how close I was to departing (stalling) the airplane, which in the A7, happens quickly and without a lot of warning. I didn't know that for much of the flight, I was outside the safe ejection envelope. And I, for sure, didn't know I had 40- foot flames coming out the tailpipe. Ironically, the one light I *didn't* have flashing at me was the ENGINE FIRE light...Now *that* might have made a difference!

The tower, I'm told, was calling for an ejection when they first saw the flames coming out the tailpipe on takeoff and me heading for the trees, but because Terry and I were both already on departure's frequency, we never heard the call. Good thing, as it turned out... The slightest encouragement and I'd have been gone.

I considered it, ejecting that is, but felt as long as I could keep it in the air, however tenuous, I'd stay with it. Dumping it into the weapons storage area didn't seem a good idea either... And I'd doubtlessly *still* be filling out paperwork.

LIFE IN THE AIR

My decision to stay with it was much debated in the weeks and months that followed that first flight. But I guess that's to be expected. Around the squadron, pilots were divided...there were sideways looks from the guys on one side and pats on the back from the guys on the other. Both sides made their case:

"He should have jumped out..." "Yea, but he saved the airplane..." "He was just lucky…"

"Yea well, you can't argue with the outcome."

"Still, it was just dumb luck, maybe...but no guts, no glory." and so on...

Fact is, getting the airplane back, by luck, skill, divine intervention...whatever, was a good thing, and kept an accident off the books for Attack Squadron 174. The skipper, now Senator John McCain, agreed and flattered me with an Air Medal with Bronze Star for outstanding airmanship. In retrospect, I'm not sure I deserved it. In fact, I probably didn't. My flight turned out OK, but I don't think a successful outcome should be the sole determinant of whether the right decision was made. Playing a long shot may work out, as it did this time, but that doesn't necessarily mean it was the right decision.

In any event, if I'd jumped out, no one would ever know for certain, if it was the right move, if I couldn't maybe have saved it...have gotten it back around. It's just one of those decisions that no matter what you do, a reasonable case could be made for doing the exact opposite. There's a lot of that in aviation. And although the advantage of hindsight is never available in real-time, there will forever be no shortage of Monday morning quarterbacks passing judgment on someone's split-second decision that they, themselves, have had a week to think about and decide. Ah well, just better to have a beer and try not to think too much of it...

NIGHT SHOT

An eerie darkness surrounds me. Not a midnight dark or a "lights out" dark but a blind dark... a claustrophobic nothingness you can feel against your cheek. I blink that I could see anything at all outside my cold cockpit home. The systems surrounding me are dead, as yet untouched by the warmth of electricity. Beneath me, a twenty-one-ton dormant airplane sways gently in perfect concert with its mother ship... a parasite and its host, insignificant on an infinite ink ocean.

Breathing is slow, easy labor against the pressure already present in my mask... my eyes dry from escaping oxygen. Preflight complete... thirty minutes till launch...I am, for now, a prisoner of time. And so, I wait...

My world is suddenly totally alive with light and sound, as my semi-dream state is shocked back to reality by glaring red lights and the static of a volume way too loud. I've obviously missed the external power signal, if indeed, one was even offered. My head pounds at the explosive intrusion, if only for a second, and I, not so silently, curse the thoughtless source outside, hidden in the night.

Electronic uproar quells; my hands move easily about the cockpit effecting their familiar tasks of readiness while my mind wanders. They say you're never as prepared for night carrier work as you are the first time, and right now, that bothers me... Can anyone ever be ready for this...I mean really ready? Will there come a day when the whole of this idea is routine? I accept the rhetorical nature of my thoughts and decide, out of necessity, that the "big picture" is just too unsettling to entertain all at once—at least for now. So, I set about concentrating on the rote... the bits... the pieces, the things I can grasp: initializing the computer, testing the Doppler, tuning the radios, and more than enough other tasks—all welcome distractions from reality.

Time's pace is picking up, and my thirty minutes are fast waning. Inertial alignment complete and engine idling at low whine, I radio my status to the below deck potentates. Meanwhile, the flight deck has come alive with a silent deliberateness...shadowed activities shrouded in a soft veil of red haze made of steam and night floodlights.

Outside my private sanctum, out of the darkness, two yellow wands flash into being, signaling imminence. The disembodied colors draw arcs of light in the night as I am marshaled forward through the stealthy maze of darkened steel to my position of final anticipation, just aft of the shuttle on the waiting bow catapult.

Two minutes and counting... movement on the flight has slowed—indicating all is in order. Now the real waiting begins. In front of me, 180 feet of insane acceleration. Aside from that, nothing... no sky...no earth...no ship. Just black...endless and sinister. Red fog appears as excess steam escapes from the cat track in front of me—a perfect touch to the macabre picture thus far painted.

One minute. Final preparations. Ram air turbine extended for emergency power, flashlight on, illuminating instruments of importance. Backups for backups. Call it paranoia, but soon, fifty feet off the ocean, eight knots above stall, IFR, in an overloaded stone of a jet... I'll need all the help I can get.

Thirty seconds. The shuttle engages my launch bar. Throttling forward, the engine howls as the Corsair hunkers down in indecision. Engine gauges dance crazily in wild overshoots of objection...reluctant repeaters of crying forces.

Fifteen seconds. Instruments checked. Controls free. Head back...throttle grip up... and finally...external lights on—the signal of ultimate readiness.

One second, the cat fires, and there is no turning back. For the next two seconds, I am the most bewildered, shocked, confused bystander that ever thought he was in control of an airplane. Seven "G"'s of shove blur my vision as I am hurled angrily and without consent into the void. Lifted from my seat, my multiplied weight is now almost totally against my back. My arms strain in amazement to control the stick and throttle while my mind boggles at the ever-increasing acceleration...150 knots...as fast as you can say it... and it's over. The acceleration quits, and I am spit into the night and dubious flight. Reality returns despite the sensory overload, and I know I've got about a tenth of a second to catch up to my airplane.

Locked on to the ADI (attitude indicator), it has my complete and undivided attention as nothing ever has. Twelve degrees nose high...hold it... cross-check angle of attack (AOA)...altimeter sags to less than 50 feet. Hold 12 degrees...12 degrees...12 degrees 12 degrees. Nothing happens. AOA is at optimum...12 degrees...

AOA... throttle bent against the stop... still nothing happens. VSI and altimeter vie for attention, not willing to accept their secondary importance.

Slowly... slowly... too slowly, the wing starts to grab. Clawing at the void, the A-7 strains to escape the evil pull of the "black hole" ocean, with only marginal success. Five hundred feet, and it still feels as if I'm at the bottom of the ocean. One thousand feet...12 degrees...12 degrees... AOA...

AOA...climbing—if you can call it that.

Two-thousand feet, breathing again... courage finally to pry my hand off the throttle long enough to raise the gear. Flaps up, and my stately climb continues as the airplane slowly accelerates through the obscurity. The night is unrelenting. Twenty thousand feet comes and goes, and still, the wet night cloud surrounds me. Invisible cumulus castles hide secretly in the dark, diffusing their lightning energy in blinding intervals, turning night into day and back again.

Twenty-five thousand feet and on top at last. I stare in awe at the scene before me. Moonlit cloudscape challenges the imagination...as stunningly brilliant as it is serene. My adrenaline-wracked body relaxes slowly under the influence of this "other world" scene as my faith in nature's compassion slowly renews itself.

For the moment, at least, I am left alone in my cockpit home. The quiet static hiss in my headset provides the sole accompaniment to the orchestral night of arcing light and silent thunder arranged for me this evening.

Reality intrudes... "Razor 24, you ready to copy your marshal instructions?" Fumbling for my mask, I stutter an affirmative, embarrassed at my inappropriate daydreaming.

"Zero-two-zero, angels twenty, push 02, say type approach requested." My voice is strangely monotone, and I feel detached... a casual observer as I watch and listen to myself read back my holding instructions to a voice in the dark. Systematically, similar orders are passed out to my compatriots above and below me, each assigned their own unique altitude and commencement or "push" time. Things seem to be running surprisingly well tonight despite Mother Nature's miserable display of temperament.

Fifteen minutes till push...more than enough time to establish myself in holding but not too much that I need to worry about fuel...or at least shouldn't need to worry about fuel. Out here, you can never be too sure. Methodically I make my way across the night sky and into my place in the holding stack. The moonlight strobes its black and white illumination of the cockpit around me while silent, static-colored clouds of dull hues race past my canopy...oblivious to the network of gray steel traffic organizing in and around them.

Reality again... "ships weather, 600 overcasts, one mile, rain." a brief pause and then... "LSO requests landing lights on".

Not a good sign, and everyone knows it. The visibility is, no doubt, worse than they're letting on. Visual acquisition of the ship's Landing Aid System (the meatball) is evidently difficult at 3/4 mile, and the ship's LSOs (landing signal officers) are taking early control until certain acquisition of the "meatball" can be had. In order to see the approaching aircraft through the rain, the LSOs require more than just our "nav" lights to go on. An unexpected twist on this, my first night of carrier "quals".

Time slips by unnoticed, and I, suddenly, find myself in a hurry to make my push time of 02. Power to military...400 knots around the holding pattern...10 seconds late on the push, and, of course, everyone knows it. Obvious to me, even at this point in my career, is that there exists in this business an obsession with precision... an "of necessity" self-demand that you learn really fast or pay the ultimate price. Pushing 10 seconds late out of holding is not, in itself, a big deal, but if it doesn't bother you, if it's "close enough" ... then you're in the wrong line of work, and rest assured, you will be accountable in a most final way.

So, down I go...10 seconds late. I leave the dreamscape above and plunge headlong into the solid gloom below. 250 knots in the descent... not 251. With only 60 seconds between aircraft on final, it doesn't take much speed differential to start bunching up aircraft on final approach, creating irrevocable confusion in CATCC (Carrier Air Traffic Control Center).

I fly automatically, oblivious to the incessant beating of rain on the plexiglass surrounding me. Threading my way methodically along an invisible pattern of bearings and altitudes, I keep a God's eye view of the approach firmly planted in my brain. Twelve hundred feet MSL and intercepting the final approach course, I impatiently await the "ACLS lock on" — the ship's guidance telemetry providing me with required bearing and glide slope information.

CATCC interrupts again... "Razor 24, go dirty at eight". They want me to hold my landing gear for eight miles, correcting for a spacing problem, I suspect. Eight miles comes up fast as I review my landing checks... gear... flaps... hook extended... landing light on... harness locked... antiskid off... cross-check angle of attack and airspeed...140 knots... about right for this fuel load. Trim and stabilize, check temps and pressures. Heavy rain thunders at me in droves, drowning out CATCC. Volume up...painfully high to hear anything at all. My concentration is at its peak now and constantly tested. Microbursts of lightning take potshots at my night vision, threatening to disrupt the necessary order and flow of things.

Inside four miles now...a late ACLS lock on. On glide slope, on centerline...rain is fierce...The cacophony of light and sound digs at my senses as I struggle to maintain my course. It has been said that a good landing is preceded only by a good approach. Nowhere is that more evident than out here. There is no 12,000-foot runway waiting at the end of this run... there can be no "big plays" in close. Unless you're on...right on at 3/4 mile, your landing is in definite jeopardy.

Approaching a mile and a half, I remain engrossed and completely occupied by my cat-and-mouse game of up-down, left-right, fast-slow. Needles are right on... I cross-check with

the heads-up display... it shows on and on. All is well, fuel is 5.5—max for landing...perfect.

Seven hundred feet, approaching one mile. Mentally calculating now: break out at 500 feet, a bit more than 3/4 mile out... at 140 knots, that's 20 seconds "on the ball", the visual approach slope indicator, and my life determinant for the final seconds of the approach.

Then... almost imperceptible through the infusion of rain and static, I hear... "Razor 24, 3/4 mile, show you on and on, call the ball". My heart skips a beat at those last three words, realizing in an instant all that is implied. This is it... the reality of the situation is thrust upon me as I look up from the intensity of instrument flying through a rain-spattered windshield. For an instant, nothing. Then, through the obscurity, it appears...My God... they can't be serious! Below the overcast, the night is an inkwell...up, down, left, and right have lost all meaning...my only clues are now supplied by the semi mirage of lights I know must be the ships VASI or "meatball".

The "ball" and its green datum lights are nothing more than blurred, runny paint smears on an impossibly black canvas. My voice surprises even me with its calm... "Razor 24, Corsair ball, 5.5" ... indicating to the LSO my fuel state and "meatball" acquisition. "Roger ball", they reply, "you're just a tad high". Sheez! I'm glad one of us can see! Slowly the resolution improves, and I am completely entranced by what I have since decided is the ultimate video game. Meatball, lineup, angle of attack...all must be perfect. Anything less, if left unchecked, will

diverge to catastrophe. Meatball, lineup, angle of attack... Over and over, the ubiquitous chant is reviewed. There is nothing else...these three things...all else is blocked.

Five seconds out now, the ship, which seemed so distant and detached heretofore, has filled my windscreen and instantly become my world. The temptation to take my eyes off the ball and look at the deck is tremendous... steel target rushing up at me at 160 mph demands attention...and still I refuse it. The ball is still my sole provider...all the way to touchdown...to take my eyes off it now could spell disaster. Time is racing...Soon...Now...

CRASH! The deck comes up hard, and my hand automatically slams the throttle to full...just in case. Any doubt is short-lived as I am slammed forward against my harness...shoulder straps digging painfully into my collarbones...DAMN!!

My composure returns not so instantly as I realize my Corsair is stopped on the deck, the number two arresting cable holding me easily at bay despite the 18,000 pounds of military

thrust still emanating from my tailpipe. My senses are overloaded as adrenaline pours into my system... Think...move...go...got to get back to the real world... Throttle idle...lights out...hook up...nose wheel steering engaged...up on the power... move, move, move...clear that foul line for the next guy and signal my status to the troubleshooters as I slide across the wet deck into the darkness just forward of the island. Mask off... stop... exhale... shaking from the rush...shaking... Time resumes a more sane pace, and I have, thankfully, a moment to relax and reflect. Only seven more to go tonight. How many in the future years, I wonder.

Turning forward into the night, I stop just aft of the number one cat, next in line to go... again...

The mix of emotions swirling through me is as foreign a thing as I have ever experienced... all blending together - blurring indistinctly until, coalescing as one, a new awareness is forged.

I can't help but wonder what lies ahead for me...what new insights await discovery, and what intimate knowledge lingers in this, most bizarre institution of higher learning.

My philosophical musing is whisked away with a sharp hand smack to the side of my airplane and the not-so-polite cursing of a taxi director too tired and too professional to put up with some young hotshot's selfish daydreaming. He turns me right and kicks me angrily to the bow cat director, who stands waiting with less sinister wands on the hip, "are you finally ready to go" pose of mild impatience. "I guess I am", I think to myself, but like I said, can anyone ever be ready for this? Two seconds later, the question is left behind in its moot little place on deck as I, once again, vanish into the night.

A NIGHT ON THE PLATFORM (PART 1)

Carrier Aviation From A Different Perspective

It's 3 A.M., and I am alone in the ready room. Slouched in my chair, I stare bleary-eyed and motionless, counting the minutes while my cigarette shrinks in one hand and my coffee grows cold in the other. My senses, dulled by fatigue, have left me isolated and unaware. My only distraction is the distant "schwunk" of the launching catapult two decks above me, and even that is barely audible through the now chronic ringing in my ears.

I've not slept for 22 hours, and I'm tired... I'm tired of *being* tired... I'm dirty, sticky, and greasy with small chunks of flight deck nonskid still stuck in my hair. I'm wet and cold with winter Mediterranean drizzle and am fighting a losing battle on two fronts against both apathy and fatigue. It hasn't been a pretty night so far on the platform, and my mental and physical being reflect all too accurately the overall miserableness of tonight's storm-tossed temperament.

I should explain at this point that tonight, I am the ship's Landing Signal Officer, or *LSO,* for the night. Aboard ship, we LSOs are called "Paddles", the name deriving from the handheld "paddle-like" signaling devices used by LSOs of the past. As LSOs, we are responsible for the safe and efficient recovery of the Carrier Airwing's aerial armada. We are there to keep the aircraft out of the water, off the ramp, and safely "in the wires". We are watchers and graders, sometimes saviors, and all the time, the guy left holding the bag should any landing go disastrously awry. Failure in this role is not an option. Mistakes are deadly and justice swift. Success, on the other hand, goes largely unrecognized as it is both expected and counted on. Interestingly, the LSO billet is held by some of the most junior aviators aboard the ship. It is a heady responsibility for so young an officer and very definitely not a job that appeals to just anyone. Right now, I muse, I'm not entirely sure it appeals to me.

The clock on the bulkhead seems to have stopped... time crawls... still 20 minutes to go. Despite my best efforts, I drift off, falling helplessly into that sleepy abyss, oblivious to times passage; my body wants only rest and cares for little else. Fortunately, and only seconds into my nascent dozing, I am roused by the faint, far away beeping of my alarm watch—dutifully announcing the approach of thirty or so tired aircraft more than anxious to get aboard and call it a night. Duty thus calls... It's time to go to work, so mustering what little energy I have left, I slough myself out of my chair, leaving my coffee and cigarette alone to continue their quiet entropic decline.

Mindlessly, I shuffle my way through the ship's below- deck labyrinth of darkened steel passageways to the catwalk just below the LSO platform at the ships aft end. I slump heavily against the small alcove's cold steel bulkhead, eyes closed and conscious of little, only distantly aware of my team's arrival. They straggle in one at a time, still wet and weary from the previous recovery, grunt their hellos, and withdraw to wait in solitude for the launch to end. Not normally so anti-social, the silence among these aviators is telling... It is plain none of us wants to be here.

On deck just above us, the noise storm of jet engines is an ongoing reminder that the landing area is still "fouled" with last- minute launches. We're early, or more likely; the launch is running late. Either way, we're not going anywhere just yet. I'm not surprised, given the horrible conditions out there tonight. Everything on deck is moving a little slower, as much because of fatigue as caution.

And so, we wait... Again... we seem to be doing a lot of that tonight.

Ten minutes and another cigarette later, the deck is still fouled, and with nowhere to go and nothing to do, my mind wanders...

The LSO platform on which I'll stand for the next hour or so is an eight-foot square piece of steel grating on the ship's port side, right alongside the landing area close to flight deck level. It's positioned just aft of the number one arresting cable, which puts it just about as far aft on the flight deck as you can "semi-safely" go. It is from this vantage point that the LSO is afforded a close-up and unobstructed view of the approaching aircraft. It is also, as we are so acutely aware of tonight, open to the elements; that is to say, outside, offering no protection or shelter at all from the weather.

Stretched across the landing area, there are four arresting cables, or "wires", and though the "three wire" is the one normally targeted by the ship's landing aid system or "lens", two or four wire "traps" are not uncommon. A one-wire engagement, on the other hand, is not a good thing and is generally frowned upon for reasons that will become obvious. You see, a perfect "on glide slope" 3-wire engagement typically results in 10 to 12 feet of vertical clearance when crossing the ramp. A one wire, on the other hand, can easily result in as little as 4 feet clearance. Throw in a pitching deck and a little late-night fatigue, and things get exceedingly dangerous in a big hurry. Suffice to say, a one-wire trap is just not the sort of thing you can repeatedly do and get away with. At least, that's how it is in the ideal world. The reality of it is that on nights like this, with its pitching decks and reduced visibility, even a one-wire can sometimes suffice to meet the environmentally lowered standards.

Overhead, the catapults are still busy with the launch, which has now run 15 minutes into the scheduled recovery time. Conditions being what they are, the delay is not really that unexpected and, to me, amounts to little more than a minor annoyance. But to the aircraft holding overhead, waiting to recover, it is much more than inconvenient. I know; I've been there. I know what it's like sitting in the holding stack, droning round and round, waiting in restless anticipation, listening anxiously while approaching times get slid again and again. With one eye on the fuel gauge and the other on the clock, you watch helplessly as your fuel-dependent comfort zone gets blown out of the tailpipe. Time is fuel... and on nights like this, fuel is priceless - quite literally, liquid insurance. To me, the delay is another cigarette... to them, it's another 500 pounds of precious fuel... 15 minutes closer to flameout... Be assured, they don't like this delay at all.

At long last, the deck above us grows quiet. The last of the launching jets Dopplers its way into the night. The launch is over... and the night, for us, begins anew...

I take a deep breath, step out onto the catwalk, and meet head-on the bitch that is the night. Black rain, accelerating sideways in 40 knots of bone-chilling wind, slap me back to full awakeness. The stinging needles of wet penetrate my meager attire as I am instantly and once again soaked and frozen to the core. Cursing under my breath, I clamor up on to the platform, slipping with every step on the greasy, rain-wet surfaces, lamenting for the nth time tonight my questionable decision to pursue this line of work.

Up on the platform and squinting through the rain, I can barely see the aircraft parked forward on the bow. Visibility is down to 1/2 mile and occasionally less as rain sweeps across the flight deck in huge sheets of zero visibility. The ceiling, almost completely obscured by the precipitation, is low, ragged and ugly. The ship's superstructure, semi-hidden in the floodlit cloud, cuts like a shark's fin through the irregular ocean of low scud, carving an almost visible groove in the low virga clawing down from the overcast.

To starboard, the rescue helicopter, ever-present during recovery, is tucked in tight formation with the ship, barely 100 feet away and right at the base of the overcast. His rotors, at times, appear to overlap the flight deck.

The view aft from the platform is a view few can appreciate. Any amount of descriptive hyperbole just doesn't do it justice. It's black dark in a way that makes you feel blind, like your eyes aren't hooked up to anything. You blink and squint, trying to find some focus... something to attach your eye to. But it's blacker than black, and there is just nothing to visually latch on to.

To my left as I face aft, the flight deck; Tonight, a hauntingly beautiful sight, one strangely out of place on this otherwise monstrous night. Lit by the nighttime floods, the rain sparkles red as it dances down the ink-wet deck, a torrent of ruby jewel rivers racing aft, waterfalling over the ramp and disappearing into the death-black void of the ocean. It's a great scene, macabre almost but one that is too beautiful to be sinister, too "other world" to be real. I should be moved by its near-supernatural beauty and would be were it not for its now "third night in a row" familiarity.

The deck is pitching, rising, and falling... fifteen feet or so... I can feel it... Like some giant low-frequency roller coaster, it pushes at me, cycling through some mysterious pattern of ups and downs and, oddly enough, left and right. The "left and rights" are the result of some fancy hydrodynamics that produces a figure eight sort of Dutch roll at the ship's aft end sweeping the landing area centerline left and right in an irregular and unpredictable fashion. Line up has thus been a major problem for the pilots tonight and, in turn, has made my job particularly challenging.

The ship's visual landing aid system—the lens or "meatball"—is 100 feet or so behind me as I face aft, alongside the landing area, and is stabilized for deck movement, but only within certain limits—limits I'm pretty sure we're exceeding right now. The effect of the pitching deck on the lens' projected glide slope is erratic and not always obvious to the landing pilots. From their perspective, it is difficult for them to "separate out" what *they're* doing as opposed to what the *pitching deck* is doing to the glide slope. That is, in part, why I'm here. I alone am in a unique position to ascertain real-time deck movement and provide the appropriate cues to the approaching aircraft.

As late and miserable as it is, there are only four of us on the platform tonight: one controlling LSO (me), one backup LSO, a writer to document each "pass" with comments and a grade, and a "phone talker" tasked with, among other things, ensuring a "clear deck" for recovery. By contrast, on a nice day, the platform is literally overflowing with spectators; some are junior LSOs trying to "train their eye", but most others are just trying to escape the below-deck claustrophobia. Tonight, not surprisingly, it is just us four ... the "have to be there" gang.

The other important figure, not physically on the platform but more so than anyone else with us in spirit, is the Air Boss. The "Boss", as he is known, a senior Carrier Aviator, is the man in the tower... the overseer of all flight deck operations and, for good or bad, my link to the senior command aboard the ship. He, more than most, wants tonight to go without incident.

The first aircraft is an F-4 Phantom, still 20 miles out. For now, he is with "CATCC" ("CAT SEE"), the Carrier's Air Traffic Control Center, and is being vectored to intercept what is essentially an ILS. The pilot then flies the ILS to a point 3/4 of a mile out, at which point he is, *in theory,* VFR and becomes my responsibility. I say *in theory* because nights at sea don't often allow VFR flying. Even after being turned over to me, he is still only quasi-visual. We joke that inside 3/4 mile, you are 90% VFR and 90% IFR. Some nights, however, the joke is just not that funny. Tonight, is one of those nights...

At 15 miles, we get one last radio check with CATCC and huddle together in the cold to await the first arrival. At 10 miles, the "Boss" calls down over the intercom, ostensibly to say hi, but I know him pretty well and can hear in his voice his more than-average concern for tonight's upcoming battle with the elements. We exchange our pleasantries, each avoiding the obvious commentary on the weather as we turn back to our respective waiting.

Five miles now, we hear eavesdropping on CATCC's transmissions. The waiting is over; my position on the platform is set; my tools of the trade are at my ready hands. In my left hand, a telephone-like handset serves as my communication link to pilots and approach control alike. And in my right hand is a "pickle", a not too easily described hand-held push button trigger sort of affair used to actuate the flashing red "wave off" lights on the ship's lens. The wave-off lights are there to mandate a go-around and exist as my last line of defense against a dangerously out-of-bounds approach. They are not something any pilot wants to see, but few have avoided.

On the flight deck, last-minute preparations are being completed as deckhands shrink into the shadows and out of the weather. A light on the console at my feet goes green, indicating a clear deck, and then red again as a last-minute straggler scurries across the landing area's "foul" line to find better shelter under the wing of a parked A-6 Intruder forward on the bow.

The approaching Phantom breaks out at 3/4 mile in good shape from what I can see through the rain. CATCC thinks so as well and hands him off to me, on glide slope, on centerline.

" Diamondback 201, Phantom Ball 5.6".

Calm... smooth, and with 5600 pounds of gas, he's right at maximum trap weight. This guy's no dope...

"**Roger** Ball Phantom", then "decks movin' a bit", I add, trying to sound bored about it. The guy is a pro... doesn't chase it... knows when it's just the deck pitching. I call for a touch of power in close as the deck comes up, but he's got it on already and slams quite profoundly on to the three-wire. For an instant, we all cringe against the onslaught of wind and rain accelerated by the Phantom's momentary full-power insurance. The three wire grabs him, screaming its arrestment, and the corralled Phantom is dragged to a violent shrieking halt.

"**Foul** deck", now while he clears the landing area and almost that quick green again. "Clear Deck!" the phone talker yells, and we are set for number two. Eyes peer aft into the void, approach frequency verified, and we listen to CATCC's final approach instructions.

I turn to the writer... "OK, no comment"; about the best grade you can get. I'll get no argument from him tonight...

Three more Phantoms come aboard with little fanfare; two "fairs" (average passes) and another "OK".

Then we get the "one" ... an A-7 Corsair at 3/4 mile, well right of centerline and LOW. Not good. I don't know how he got there and don't really care. In any event, I don't wait for the CATCC handoff... "Paddles Contact, Corsair", I say, taking visual control and silencing CATCC; "You're LOW". My inflection is important here - I'm not excited, but he needs to know I'm serious. I want to come across intense, sort of mad, with a little impatience thrown in there. Let him fly the aircraft though; don't make the correction for him. Tell him what, not how... You jump in too soon, and they'll quit flying. There is still time for him to fix this, so let him fly it. The power comes on. He's responding... good. "Now, line it up". Again, don't make the correction for him.

He's approaching the in-close position and again sags low... a green angle of attack light flickers on his nose gear... indicating a slower-than-optimum condition. He's underpowered and slow to react... a dangerous combination... time to jump in... "POWER," I call. Translation; "Add power NOW, I don't care if you don't think you need it, DO IT ANYWAY!" Well, the flickering green light goes steady, and the airplane sags still lower.

He's still not responding, and the airplane's angle of attack is getting dangerously high. "POWER, POWER!" I demand, with increasing volume and intensity. I mean to sound angry now and my finger tightens on the pickle switch. I can feel my body tensing—rising up on the balls of my feet... focus narrowing... Watch him... watch him... Slowly, reluctantly, The A-7 responds, but not enough... He inches up, ever so slightly, and just barely pokes his nose up into the center of the glide slope. My body still tense... it isn't over yet... Then, his engine sighs... the death knell... he hangs there, motionless by illusion and suspended, I know, by the most tenuous of threads! I can see by the light triangle of his position lights he's getting critically slow, and I know why... He's sucked the power off, fearful of flying up through the glide slope! DAMN! Alarm bells go off in my head, screaming disaster!! I don't wait to see what I know is coming... "WAVEOFF, WAVEOFF, WAVEOFF!!!" I demand. Microseconds later, the airplane quits flying and turns to stone. Damn! Damn! Damn! He's settling fast and just outside the wave-off "window". I mash the pickle in adrenaline reaction and light the deck, myself, and a way too cocked up A-7 in pulsating red wave-off lights. He has yanked his nose up, way up, in a vain attempt to halt his descent. The aircraft is teetering on the verge of a full-blown departure stall! I can almost hear its wing tearing at the wind, bending it through impossible angles while his engine roars in desperation, helplessly imprisoned—trapped crying behind the power curve. Time has slowed to a standstill. Adrenaline courses through my system at breakneck speed! My mind is racing, thinking a thousand thoughts, seeing a thousand things, and getting nowhere. WAVEOFF! WAVEOFF! WAVEOFF!! my volume distorted yells continue. He's drifting towards us, but I don't dare try and line him up at this point—his grip on the air is dubious as it is. I can't believe he's even still flying! He's making a beeline for the platform at nearly deck level growing bigger and more menacing

with each flash of wave-off lights. My hand is a frozen death grip on the pickle. I'm yelling my drowned-out "WAVEOFFS" into the handset, staring at this Godzilla-like form as if, by sheer force of will, I could keep him from hitting the ramp in front of me. My compatriots, loyal to this point, bail into the net alongside the platform and roll to comparative safety in the catwalk beneath me. I alone remain, transfixed by the display of aeronautical impossibility... desperate to keep him in the air. He's gigantic in my field of view, his underside planform looming larger and larger with each passing instant. I mean, he is RIGHT

THERE!! Common sense screams at me to jump... to leave the platform before it's too late, but my feet are glued to the deck. I just *can' t* let this happen! Not me! Not this time! Not now! Waveoff!! Waveoff!! Waveoff!! because there is just nothing else to say...

The next "time expanded" seconds seem to take forever, but eventually, the tender balance of "will he/won't he" finally tips, and to my complete amazement and despite a grotesquely nose-high attitude, the Corsair clears the platform. His 15000 pounds of thrust hit me from 30 feet or so, and I am thrown to my knees, clawing blindly at the steel grating, trying to keep myself from being blown overboard. Wind and rain whip across me with hurricane force… Errant phone cords are flailing in the blast, hammering the grating around my head, struggling to break free. In the midst of all this, squinting through the grating below me, I can see my compatriots; huddled together like frightened stowaways in some pitch-darkened cargo hold, each with eyes wide and mouths open, agog with ridiculously identical expressions of frozen disbelief. Funny, even then, I nevertheless remind myself to laugh about it later… assuming there is a later…

With the tempest still raging around me, I turn to follow the Corsair with my eyes as he staggers howling forward across the angle deck. Stinging rain accelerated by the Corsair's exhaust rips at my face, but still, I watch mesmerized as the A-7, now in nearly full planform view, evaporates slowly into the night, with a floodlight red cloud of high lift condensation almost completely covering the top of the wing.

Grabbing one of the now subdued handsets, I radio, "Watch your attitude", and sound so absurdly nonchalant that I actually laugh at the sound of myself in two-second retrospect.

My body's reaction, lagging seconds behind times, eventually catches up with things and floods my system with several gallons of "fight or flight" chemistry. My heart is slamming inside my chest, and my head is throbbing with a massive adrenaline overload. I pace furiously back and forth, cussing a continuous string of four-letter expletives in part because I'm angry at myself for letting him get so far out of whack, but mostly just to try and dissipate some of my sudden energy rush.

In time, my crew collects themselves back on the platform, not the least bit embarrassed at their auspicious retreat and only somewhat dismayed at having missed the front-row view of the near miss—

nevertheless, the dichotomy of before and after is plainly evident. The miserable conditions are, at least temporarily, ignored. Certainly, no one is tired anymore. Our brush with disaster has left us all wired, jumping around pointlessly with restless energy like a bunch of Ritalin-starved third graders.

My animated description of the "almost" ramp strike is cut short by the Boss 'timely reminder that the next aircraft is approaching 3/4 mile. As if on cue, another A-7 pops out of the dark at 3/4 mile in good shape and completely unaware of the previous excitement, thanks to CATCC's alternating approach frequencies.

Back concentrating on the business at hand, I watch the next 5 or 6 come aboard in pretty rapid succession. Nothing dramatic, but still one right after the other, bam, bam, bam. CATCC has got 'em bunched pretty close together tonight, an efficient operation, to be sure, but not entirely a good thing, especially tonight. You see, because of the slippery conditions on deck, airplanes are understandably moving more slowly while exiting the landing area. That, along with CATCC's minimum separation, has us running the risk of "fouled deck" wave-offs. Take it from me; The last thing any pilot wants to do tonight is to go around. The idea of abandoning a perfectly good approach, schlepping back around the pattern, blowing precious fuel out the tailpipe, and then having CATCC try and squeeze you back into a hole on final with 1000 pounds less fuel than the first time is something no pilot out here looks forward to and no LSO wants to deal with.

The frenzied pace out here is all consuming and has left us little time to think about the "one". It's odd that such an extreme moment goes forgotten, but that's the way it is. Rapid fire action, and when from time to time the action gets extreme, time doesn't stop to let you bask in the moment. Aircraft are arriving in 60-second intervals, and each can potentially need me to pull their butt out of a jam. It sounds cliché, I know, but I owe them nothing less than my complete and undivided attention.

Finally, a break in the action, a hole in the pattern—probably vectoring our wave-off back into the lineup. Thankfully, the rain has let up somewhat, and I make visual contact at a mile. He looks good, maybe a tad high, and at 3/4 mile makes his call; " 421 Corsair ball, 3.2".

" Roger ball Corsair, deck is steady, work it in the center "—a not-so-subtle implication that he is not quite on the ideal glide slope and that the deck, at least for now, is not moving around too badly. I say it as if I have completely forgotten about his last pass. I haven't, of course, and he knows it, but I try to make it sound routine, nevertheless. He's high and goes higher - as tough a thing for him to correct as it is for me to help him too. A dangerous place to be, high like that, particularly in close. The Corsair, because it's got no usable speed brake in the landing configuration, is already way back on the power. Any further power reduction puts its big fan engine in a critically slow acceleration range, and often, by the time you realize the need for power, it's too late. Besides, even if he does catch it just right, coming down off the high, his necessarily high descent rate, coupled with an out-of-phase pitching deck, could result in a damagingly hard impact.

In any case, he's taking no chances. He stays high, too high, and in close, I send him around. The Boss has, of course, been keeping track of things and calls down.

" What do you think, Paddles? You gonna catch this guy?"

" We'll get him, Boss; he's just a little gun-shy right now." A two-second pause then, "how bout we send him to the Tanker to think about it?"

" Good idea, he's gettin' a little low on gas, and "Sig" just went "WOXOF".

Damn... The weather at Sigonella, Italy, our divert field, has just gone zero zero.

"Gee Boss, you're just full of good news..." "Just get him"

"Roj"

Time goes by... The rain is unrelenting. We are soaked to the bone and visibly shaking in the cold, gale-force wind. The rest of the 30 or so aircraft arrive with varying degrees of aplomb but none particularly outrageous. We are left with only two; the Tanker (another A-7, as it happens, configured to give out fuel) and our guy.

We haven't heard anything out of CATCC lately, and the four of us on the platform are growing increasingly impatient, waiting for our last two planes to show up. The adrenaline high has worn off, and the night's weariness is starting to take its toll. With renewed apathy, we've withdrawn from one another, each trying in his own way to deal with the misery and each, I suspect, not really succeeding.

In the midst of all this, Mother Nature throws us a bone... The ceiling comes up some, or the visibility improves, hard to say which, but either way, we start to feel better about things. That is, until the Boss calls down.

"Uh, Paddles."

"What's up, Boss?"

"421 was unable Tanker rendezvous; clouds are solid to 40,000."

"Great... How much has he got?" "Couple... Maybe three passes."
"Shit."

A NIGHT ON THE PLATFORM (PART 2)

The four of us are still trying to digest the Boss' report when the writer spots our guy in and out of the scud about a mile out. After a frantic scramble to tune the correct frequency, we are set just in time to hear the ball call.

" 421 Corsair ball, 2.2". " Roger ball Corsair".

He's dead on and flies an absolutely picture-perfect pass to a touchdown just prior to the three-wire. We are all thus more than surprised when he rolls straight off the angle deck and back into the night.

" Bolter, Bolter, Bolter" I call. (As if he doesn't realize he's missed). I throw in an obligatory "Rotate" as he clears the angle deck just to be sure he's headed up and turn to my crew.

" He looks good to you guys?".

" Yeas" all around. "Attitude look OK?" (Sometimes a nose-down attitude will raise the tailhook enough for it to skip over the wires).

Again, the platform agrees that all looked well. Oh well, just one of those things, I guess... but a deep-down feeling makes me not so sure. It could be the hook has somehow lost its "snubber" pressure - the precharge that keeps it held firmly in the down position. I hope not. We've all seen that before and know that it can sometimes take four or five passes to "get lucky" and grab a wire. Tonight, and with his fuel state, we just don't have the time.

Replaying his last pass in my mind and being the pessimist I sometimes have to be, I am haunted by an all too familiar sense of uneasiness. Things are heading in a very uncomfortable direction, and I don't like it. The others on the platform are strangely quiet, I suspect, for the same reason. I try to brush aside my growing angst, but it's no use. Suddenly I'm not so tired anymore. My mind has already shifted gears readying itself for the unknown, trying to stay ahead of things. I instinctively start playing the "what if" game, weighing options, reviewing possibilities, and hoping at the same time it won't come to any of those things.

It's going to take about 15 minutes for 421 to be vectored back around. With nothing for us to do right now, the 15 minutes seem to take forever. But as uncomfortable as it is for us, I know that it's got to be worse for him. Droning around down low, his fuel is fast waning, and he knows there is no airborne fuel or divert option. He's got to get aboard. And he's got to do it soon.

Eventually, he's back around.

" 421 Corsair ball 1.2".

" Roger Ball Corsair", and then as an aside... Hook-skip last time, watch your attitude in the wires".

I say it with all the steely nerve nonchalance that I can muster. But inside I'm thinking... 1.2! 1.2!? That's 1200 pounds!! You gotta be kidding me!! Shit!! This guy's out of gas!!

A virtual replay of the last pass is presented to us, including, unfortunately, the hook-skip part. Things are now officially serious, and everyone knows it. The ship has come alive with discussion, readiness, and worry. Inputs are coming in from all over. The "com" channels are all of a sudden jammed with chatter. The plane guard helo, the airborne tanker, the Boss, CATCC, and we on the platform are busy running potential scenarios through in our minds. We have little to choose from, and even the most optimistic of us have some serious doubts.

The gravity of the situation is suddenly upon us... this is the real deal, and things are not looking good. He has got one more shot at the deck, and unless we can get him rendezvoused with the Tanker, he'll be out of gas and stuck with only a few options, none of them very appealing.

Someone, somewhere, talks about flying him into the barricade. It sounds, at first, like a reasonably good idea, but it carries with it its own set of hazards. Besides, because rigging the barricade essentially closes the deck, we'd have to take the Tanker first, thus leaving no option at all for airborne fuel and an almost guaranteed flameout should the problem aircraft fail to get aboard. Further, the unfavorable working conditions on the flight deck make it unlikely the barricade could even be rigged in the little time we have remaining. The barricade option is dismissed pretty quickly.

The other option is a controlled ejection... Over water... at night... in these seas... yeah, right... Nobody even wants to think about that.

My job has just gotten seriously difficult. I am acutely aware of this. I've got to get this guy aboard; that much is certain - with or without his help. I may have to break some rules and work him closer to the edge. If he is out of bounds, I'll have to get him back in bounds. If he is unsafe... well, that's the tricky part. A wave-off effectively guarantees a flameout, but on the other hand, letting an unsafe approach continue inside the wave-off point is the biggest "no no" in the book and is unquestionably the most dangerous thing an LSO can let happen. There's a flight deck full of people and airplanes I have to think about.

This is the quintessential "fluid event" where the rules are written real-time; followed one second, thrown out the next, always changing, ever flexible as events unfold. The situation is not good, and I don't like it; I don't like it at all. One minor error, and we've got a catastrophe of devastating proportions.

Time is running out. A decision must be made quickly. If he hook-skips again, we're screwed.

After some consternation, we decide on a rather unorthodox course of action. Nobody really likes it, but we all agree that it's the only way. It's decided to have 421 attempt a rendezvous with the Tanker *under* the overcast. This is way tricky and requires that a lot of dangerous and difficult things come together in an amazingly precise way. Under the overcast, it's as black IFR as you can get. You're on the gauges, or ought to be. There is no up or down, no horizon, and at 400 feet, a two-second distraction can kill you. There is no margin, no second chance... you screw up at all, and you're dead.

The plan is to take the Tanker first and wave him off when he gets in close. He then, while essentially IFR and using the ship as his only visual cue, must position himself in a dangerously low, beneath the overcast circuit around the ship and play it so that he is just ahead of the ship and close aboard when the low fuel Corsair crosses the ramp. That way, should the Corsair bolter again, the Tanker would be in an ideal position for the join-up (if any position can be considered ideal on a night like this).

Now, here's where the real fun starts... The subsequent rendezvous and fuel transfer are critically difficult events. "Plugging in", sometimes elusive even under ideal conditions, is going to be a real bear tonight. Vertigo is at its meanest out there, just itching to strike... and time, or rather "lack thereof," is pressuring everyone to hurry everything, cutting safety margins to virtually zero and effectively mandating perfection from everyone involved. The stress of knowing this is a do-or-die thing doesn't help either.

The Tanker pilot's job is particularly exacting and crucially important. In fact, he is the key to pulling this thing off. First, assuming the rendezvous goes without incident (and that's no small assumption), he has got to manage the refueling panel—a notoriously poorly lit black box hidden beneath his left elbow and just about the most awkward thing to see and deal with and still stay right side up. He cannot afford even a micro second lapse of attention. Further, and with virtually no room for error, he must smoothly and precisely maneuver the tanking formation back around and on to the final... utilizing only the ship's TACAN and whatever visual reference he's able to eke out, at 200 feet, at night, in the rain... alone. Oh, and did I mention there is no autopilot?

His concentration is being yanked in a dozen different directions at once, each requiring 110% of his attention. He is alone in that aircraft and has got one awesome responsibility: one bitch of a task. I don't envy him for his job. We "single seat" types are characteristically proud of our one man / one airplane status, but I'll bet you anything our Tanker pilot would give up some "single seat" pride in exchange for another pair of eyes on board with him tonight. I know I would.

The Tanker is first to show up, as planned, and I send him around with a brief shot of wave-off lights at 1/2 mile. He cleans up and heads up the starboard side of the ship, right at the bases of the clouds. We watch him turn left and cross the bow. He's listening to approach now, gauging his turn back around, timing his pattern, and playing his turn to set up a nearly impossible rendezvous with the low-fuel Corsair, who is now on his approach somewhere aft of the ship.

The Tanker is barely visible as he passes abeam, winking in and out of the scud at what appears to be an impossibly low altitude. CATCC calls our guy 12 miles out.

The next two minutes seem like a lifetime. All is quiet on the platform as everyone searches for signs of the two aircraft. The rain is falling in sheets, and no one seems to notice. CATCC calls 421 at 1 mile. We can hear the Tanker acknowledging CATCC's reports but still see no sign of either. At 3/4 mile, we get the handoff. For a long second, we see nothing. Then a jumble of lights starts to materialize out of the gloom on final, just an obscure blob of color, really too indistinct to make out anything. I hate to bug em', but I need more than that to go on if I'm going to take him any further.

" Guys, I need your landing lights ".

Almost simultaneously, two bright lights flash on. I'm at once impressed and amazed at the near-perfect position the Tanker has achieved. He's got it wired! I can't figure out for the life of me how he managed to put himself in such a beautiful position, but there he sits, in perfectly matched formation not two wingspans away as if without a care in the world. Just inside 1/2 mile, he slides away and eases ahead of the low-fuel Corsair.

Our boy is looking good and sounds steady.

" 421 Corsair Ball, uh... point five".

" Roger Ball Corsair, Tanker will be at your high one o'clock if you need im'".

The guy's on rails. Dead center glide slope. He knows when you gotta be good.

I see the slow light blink for just a second as he goes by me, "setting the hook", and watch as he slams down on the deck. The hook touches down just prior to the two wires, and for the first time, I can actually see it bouncing over the 2, 3 and 4 wires. DAMMIT!

" BOLTER, Bolter, hook skip!"

He's airborne and turning almost before he clears the angle deck, locked on to the Tanker who has positioned himself exquisitely just 300 feet above and to his right with the refueling drogue already extended. They come together almost

immediately and disappear just as quickly from view with the plane guard helo in hot pursuit.

The radios are deathly silent. The *real* waiting begins... We manage only an occasionally glimpse at the two as they make their way back around the pattern. I seriously doubt our guy's got the fuel to make it all the way around, but if the Tanker pilot is sharp, he is going to give the fuel-critical A-7 every chance just in case he's unable to get plugged in. My bet is he'll drag him all the way around the pattern if he has to, set him up for a long low final, and give him one last shot at the deck.

The scene on the flight deck is as surreal as it gets. Personnel all over the flight deck are frozen in position. Somehow everyone knows the whole story. All eyes are locked on the two aircraft mushing their way through the night, waiting for the telltale flash of ejection seat rockets and praying it doesn't happen.

The silence on the frequency is deafening while everyone awaits word of a successful "plug". We listen anxiously as CATCC calls the base leg vector. I don't like it. We should have heard something by now. He's got to be out of gas or vaporously close to it.

The plane guard helo is back alongside the ship to assume its starboard station. I can see two rescue swimmers sitting in the open door, suited up and ready to go. Things are not looking good.

They're at a mile. We still can't tell what's happening, and the frequency is obstinate in its silence. I like to think I'm ready for anything, but still, it would be nice to hear something... anything. I need to know if I'm gonna have to take him or not.

They roll out on the final. The Tanker has positioned the two right on the center line and in level flight; they are approaching the glide slope from below. At 3/4-mile, CATCC hands them off.

" 421 and flight, you are well below glide slope, on the centerline, call the ball".

Silence...

" Paddles Contact", I say, "You're low".

They know it, of course, but I say it anyway just to let them know I'm here. Still, there is silence... My finger is poised on the wave-off lights as they approach 1/2 mile ... This is cutting it way too close... I can't take them much further without "com". Dropping protocol, I beg,

" Come on guys... Talk to me... I can't take you much closer".

" Uh... Standby Paddles". Then another voice,

" OK... I'm in".

" Roger that, standby" ... then, "Paddles, we have good transfer... We're going around".

The emotional release on the flight deck is almost palpable. Cheers erupt all around as pent-up emotions are released from held breaths. Even we four on the platform, uncharacteristically awestruck, stare with embarrassed wonder at the scene before us.

Lit intermittently by the Tanker's pulsating red beacon, the two gray ghosts roar majestically past the ship's island, connected to one another by the thin life-sustaining umbilical. It's a great scene... The low-fuel Corsair is snuggled right up to the Tanker. Separated by less than 10 feet, he's got the refueling drogue pushed all the way up into the Tanker's store. Right now, staying "plugged in" is a life-or-death thing, and he, better than anyone, knows it.

As great as this all is, it is only a minor victory, really... The successful refueling has bought us some time, but the essential difficulty remains. We still have a major problem trying to get this guy aboard, only now, because the Tanker has depleted his reserve, and we have *two* low-fuel aircraft on our hands.

There is not much we can do with the "hook-skip" airplane that we haven't already tried. The "snubber" or gas pressure holding the arresting hook firmly in the down position has somehow depleted, and recharging can only be done on deck. The on-deck alert Tanker, we have been advised, is down with a hydraulic leak, and the airborne Tanker from the previous launch is "sour" with a drogue problem. There is no gas left, and time once again has us on the run. We probably have time to try the barricade now, but only as a last resort.

We decide, instead, to try a rather unorthodox procedure first—one I don't think the Carrier Suitability Team ever dreamed of. We know that if we can prop the arresting wires up a few inches higher, it may help the hook to engage even if it's bouncing. It's a good idea in concept, and if we had two or three hours to think about it, we could probably come up with some pretty decent ways to do it. But of course, we don't... We've got to do something now. We've got to try *something*. But what? The Boss actually comes up with something simple and clever that might just be the answer.

After a brief consultation with him, I turn to the phone talker, "Sammy, go down below deck and grab as many rolls of toilet paper as you can carry... <u>move it</u>!" He looks at me like I'm from Mars but hurries off anyhow, shaking his head. While Sammy's gone, I explain the plan to the others on the platform. Sammy's back quicker than I would have thought, with about 8 rolls. We each grab a couple and scramble up onto the flight deck. Leaning heavily into the 40-knot wind, we jam the rolls sidewise under the 3 and 4 wires. They raise some parts of the sagging wires just a bit, maybe an inch or two, but every little bit helps, but as this *is* a game of inches, we are hoping it will make the difference. It's a crazy thing, I know, but we're out of ideas, and the barricade scenario on a pitching deck scares everyone. It might as well give him one more shot, however weird it may seem.

We try and take the Tanker first, but he refuses, stubbornly determined to stay available just in case. He can't have much more fuel to give out and is deliberately putting himself in a potentially dangerous position. It's a gutsy move, as any more fueling will leave him critically low. Still, he's got a good hook and, thus, a better shot at getting aboard.

Refueling complete, the freshly fueled Corsair has made his way back around. At 3/4 mile, we can see him with the Tanker once again hanging motionless just off his wing. This is *the* critical pass. The weather is as severe as it's been tonight. The rain is unrelenting, and the sea state is rougher than ever. The deck is pitching in big irregular cycles. I try unsuccessfully to figure out the pattern of its movement and, finally, just give up. As with most things tonight, Mother Nature is exhibiting a cruel flair for the dramatic.

The ship is making minimum steerage, about 10 knots. Even still, the wind across the deck is close to 50. The ship has been hunting, steering a little left, a little right, trying to keep the wind down the angled deck, but I can see from the pennants flying on the island that right now, the wind is axial, that is, down the length of the ship. Because of this and given the geometry of the angled flight deck, there is produced, in effect, a right crosswind. The high wind also reduces the "on glide slope" ramp clearance to less than 10 feet. These and myriad other factors are racing through my mind. I try desperately to think of everything… I must. As much as I would like to believe otherwise, a successful outcome rests largely on my shoulders.

Over the intercom, I call the Boss to have him shift the lens to a steeper four-degree glideslope, a procedure regularly used to increase the hook-to-ramp clearance in high winds.

" Already done Paddles".

The Boss is right on top of things, and I can tell from his voice that he's as stoked as any of us.

At 3/4 mile, we get the handoff …

" 421 show you on and on, call the ball".

" 421's Clara".

Damn! It's the rain! He can't see the ball.

" Roger that Corsair, you're lookin' good right now… just slightly right and correcting … You should pick up a ball any second".

" 421's got a ball 2.3".

" Roger Ball Corsair, don't go high", I hurry to add, sensing a bit too much power. "Fly it down now, nice and easy". He comes down off of the high in close and goes slow trying to stop his descent with his nose.

" A little power back on" and then "You're Home," a not-so-subtle code to let him know he has crossed the ramp.

" Attitude!, Attitude!", a last-second double-check to have him set the hook and not drop his nose.

The deck comes up, and the Corsair crashes down hard on the 2 wire. Wet toilet paper confetti showers the deck aft of the roaring airplane. I squint, blinded against the onslaught of paper, rain, and nonskid, to see if he traps. The hook touches down hard and rebounds, smacking into the fuselage's underside. Time is moving in super slow motion. Snapshot-like stills flash sequentially, each teasingly incomplete. The hook falls again as the Corsair blasts over the 3 wire. DAMN! The engine is spooling for the anticipated bolter, and my redundant "ATTITUDE" calls are lost in a 130-decibel wall of sound. Everyone is fearing the worse. People are frozen in position. A thousand breaths are held! It's as if the scene is purposely being played out for maximum effect by someone with a bizarre sense of melodrama. The airplane is already rotating as the main gear roll over the 4 wire. "JESUS!! ¡¡COME ON!!" I yell into the wind, a desperate plea to force things my way. All of a sudden, the Corsair's nose slams down, rotated violently by some monstrous deceleration while a screaming 4 wire is yanked to near full extension halfway down the angle deck.

WE GOT HIM! WE GOT HIM!" the writer yells. Cheers explode from the guys on the platform, jumping up and down in what would at any other time be an embarrassing display of very *un*macho emotion. All across the flight deck, people are blasted out of their frozen reverie. They come alive again, instantly active, moving all of a sudden in hyper-motion quickness to guide the Corsair clear of the foul line and reset the deck for the next arrival.

I feel the congratulatory pounding on my back, but I just don't have the energy left to partake in the jubilation. I am wasted... emotionally and physically drained. The rain washes over my face and my arms hang limp at my side. I watch absently as the Corsair clears the gear and moves forward out of the landing area. Adrenaline headache number two arrives on schedule, pounding inside my skull and obliterating any sense of relief I may even think about feeling.

My inappropriate daydreaming has me almost missing the Tanker's call at 3/4 mile. He's dangerously low on fuel and is undoubtedly the most tired person out here. He's been airborne for almost three hours and engaged for most of that time in some of the most exhaustingly demanding flying imaginable. I turn to the writer, "If he even gets aboard, it's an "OK"... Got it?"

The Tanker's pass is not perfect. A little of this, a little of that... I call for a little "right for lineup" at the ramp to drop him down off the high, and he crashes down quite unceremoniously on the three wire.

My last plane is home, safe if not sound, and for me, the night is at last over. On the flight deck and around the ship, everything is back to normal. Just like that... People shift gears and, like little automatons, go about their familiar tasks as if nothing at all has happened. No pomp, no circumstance, the night is forgotten, ho-hum, la dee da... already a thing of the past, and everyone is all of a sudden tired again, hungry again, bored again. How strange ...

And so, it goes... The sun's pink glow on the horizon bodes well for the next recovery, but it is of little consolation to me after my seemingly endless night of misery. I pass the handset to my well-rested relief, just arriving for the next shift and relax, allowing for the first time tonight my body's well-earned submission into exhaustion. I must be quite a sight if my relief's first reaction is any indication. He looks at me with equal degrees of pity, fright and wonder. "Rough night?" he says with typical aviator sarcasm.

"Yea, rough night", I respond, along with a few other unprintable words.

I decide to skip the debrief and hope everyone understands. I make my way to my stateroom and crash face down onto my rack, still fully clothed. I'm wet and cold, and I can't remember when I've been so completely wiped out. Yet strange as it is, I have this thought, this indisputable truth that right now, there is no place I'd rather be and no job I'd rather be doing. I know it's absurd, it's ridiculous, and it doesn't make any sense, but still, it is undeniable. I chuckle inwardly at the truth of it and try to make sense of the apparent contradiction.

Sometimes the game out there is as fulfilling a challenge as I can imagine. An all-out life on the edge contest. A contest of skill and wits, of chance and odds, where you get no points for second place as success is too often measured in life and death terms. As fantastic as it all is, I sometimes wonder if I don't take the whole experience for granted. It's easy to do sometimes. Because the daily routine out here is just that, a day-in and day-out routine, you get used to the everyday excitement, the constant thrill of it all. You think you've seen it all, and then along comes a night like this, a special night, when the near-heroic professionalism of a ship full of people pull together to allow the nearly impossible to be done as if it's an everyday thing and you are reminded with poignant clarity what it is all about. What this life is all about. It's as if life itself was *designed* for these moments; The world - an action stage set for the performance of a lifetime. How fortunate are we to be the lucky participants.

LIFE IN THE AIR

YOYO TANKER

There is something about exhaustion that makes sleep so perfect. Throw in the gentle swaying of the ship beneath you and the darkness that only 3 decks down can bring, and it's nigh on perfect. And so, it was for me. Almost... Round-the-clock ops. Three AM, and just now getting to bed. Drifting off, deeper...deeper... almost gone...sweet exhaustion...

Then.... Brring!!... Brring!!... Brring!!... I'm shocked out of my nascent reverie by the phone's obnoxious intrusion. Ignore it.... Ignore it...it stops... sweet...

Two minutes...

Knock, knock, knock...

"Rocket, you in there...? Nothing... don't answer... ignore... louder... BAM, BAM, BAM!!

" Yo Rocket!, Get up!" ...

Wha... Grog... What the... shit... "Go Away!!"

" Rocket, get your butt up; they need you to take the Yo-Yo Tanker".

"What!? Who??! I just landed... I'm not flyin' anything!...

That's Boomer's hop anyway" ...

" Boomer's got an ear block, and you and the Skipper are the only ones night current".

" Great, let the Skipper take it..." (like that'll happen).

" Very funny".

" Come on , I'm wiped."

" Sorry dude, Skipper says you're it."

Crap...

And thus, my adventure began. Three AM aboard the Aircraft Carrier Independence, somewhere in the middle of the Mediterranean, out of a dead sleep. I had just landed. Round-the-clock ops... too much flying, too much weather, not enough rest... This will be my third flight in 12 hours, and I am exhausted... Well, I was, until this. Right now, I'm too pissed off to be tired... That'll wear off...

YoYo Tanker. Great... Oh well... Super quick thirty-minute flight... up and down, Hence the name. Over before you know it. Give the Phantoms three grand apiece and beat feet back aboard... might even catch the tail end of the late movie... Maybe it won't be so bad... yea, right... who am I kidding... weather sucks... rain, pitching deck, and all that... whatever...

Gotta get up, gotta do it... get up, come on, get up. Ugh... groan, fumble, fumble, light switch... click, yaa! bright... Blinded... kick, stumble... flight suit and boots...Splash of cold water to wake up... not working...

To the paraloft... deserted passageways... dim red lights... dull hum of sleeping electronics... like some sort of ghost ship...

There. Suit up... "G" suit. Stupid on a Tanker hop... damn zippers... Torso harness, survival vest, emergency radio. I wonder when that was last checked. I'll hope it works. Flashlight... now that I'll check. You never know... Helmet bag and kneeboard... Loaded down... Pen... pen... where's my pen? "Hey Wallace, lemme steal your pen..."

Out the door... Trip over the knee knocker on the way out... not happy...

Trudge, slog and trudge... Down the passageway, quick

swing through the ready room... Launch brief still on the tube. The weather sucks... big surprise...

Position - 150 miles south of Sigonella, Italy. Doesn't mean much to me... less, of course, I have to divert... Right... I don't think so... That's all I need...

Escalator to the flight deck... broken again... Up I slog... three decks... clomp, clomp, cuss and sweat... Damn ship... Flight deck at last. Helmet on, cuss some more...deep breath... out I go... into the night...

Cold, wet, black, dark... red... fog... mist... still and quiet except for the clang bang of tiedown chains and tow bars... shadowed forms moving in slow motion... vis worse than I thought... and rain...

My KA-7 Corsair, Tanker configured, already spotted on Cat I. I'll be the first to go... Got to be in order to do my thing and make the recovery that's already holding overhead. The normal cycle for non-yoyo's is 2.5 hours... YoYo is busy... busy... busy.... let me tell you. And just me and no autopilot to do it... black night... that too...

Preflight in the rain. All's well, just the usual hydraulic leaks. Raining harder... drippin down the back of my neck... yuck... Sure, 'd be nice to "down" the bird... a quick "no-fly" write up and back to bed... aah... course, I'd never hear the end of it... Something keeps me on track.

In the cockpit, Airman Alvarez helps me get settled.

" Go on, Mo... I got it, go stay dry..."

" Thanks, Lt... have a good one..." He's gone...

Canopy closed. Locked, over center clunk... quiet... drip, drip, drip... sigh...

External power... Yah! Lights and static... turn 'em down... eyes adjusting... fumble with my mask... a couple of drags on the O2 to wake up...

Prestart checks... set things up... hands moving automatically... flip, twist, dial, set, and check... couple of more swigs on the O2...

Crank it... Whrrr... thud... whoosh... whine and idle... Up and running...

Post-start. Test this, stow that, ready these, adjust those, calculate weights and figure speeds... what am I forgetting? I guess nothing... 20 min to launch... alignment is coming along... more O2...

Mission... Got to fuel the Phantoms overhead at 15k... two of em '... three grand apiece ... not sure what for... night like this... no real mission for them... hang on the blades, "max conserve" for two hours... throw yourself at the back of the ship and say you did it... oh well... mine is not to reason why...

Boomer better not be watching the movie... I'll kick his butt... 5 minutes... 37 thou' on the weight board... should be a nice shot tonight... now that oughta wake me up...

Gettin' close. Last minute things... Extend the "Rat" (emergency electrical power) ...just in case... Yeah... the "Rat" ... Gets me thinking... Single generator... one engine... no battery backup...young and stupid - that's us .... Try not to think about it...

Clip the flashlight ...clicked on and aimed at the ADI (attitude indicator) ... just in case... Arm the ejection seat..........just in case... and for sure, don't think about that...

One minute... a quick little prayer... just in case...

30 seconds... Launch bar engages... throttle up. Engine howls... gauges look good... controls free... relaxed... time to go... lites on, head back… let's do it!!

BANG!!!SLAM!!!WHOOSH... Spat!! UGH! Damn! good

shot, good shove, rotate...settle... rotate, settle some more... rotate... rotate, ...12 degrees on the ADI... angle of attack is optimum... ADI, come on... climb you bitch... climb... radar altimeter beeps its 40-foot warning... pig Tanker... clawing up now... barely... gear up, ADI 12 degrees, AOA checks... thousand feet... accelerate... flaps up. Two thousand... exhale... 250 knots bending it back overhead... in the clag... Phantoms goin' off right behind me... one off the waist and one off the bow... 15 thou'-solid... 12 was ok... back down.

"Diamondbacks, Texaco. I'll see you at angels

12...15s clobbered" ...

Port orbit, 220 knots... Extend the drogue. Wait...

Phantom number one's black silhouette slides aboard handsomely... I kill my beacon when he gets close...Silently floating... Looks like a black needle out there. A sinister red glow from the cockpit... like something out of Star Wars... Death Drone or some such thing... " Cleared in"...

Airspeed... hold 220... The stone jet Phantoms they get antsy, anything slower. Some minor fencing goes on between the Phantom and the basket, but eventually, he's in… "green light" ... good transfer. Gallons ticken off on the meter. well, I think they are anyway... hard to see... twist and turn to see under my left arm... tryin' to stay right side up... console lights suck... black box almost unreadable... why'd they put it there... damn engineers... watch the airspeed... power up just a hair... how many gallons is three grand anyway? Oh yea---------...mind's slow... stay alert... almost done... airspeed... be smooth...

Here comes Phantom #2... Yikes!! Way too much closure... FOOOSHT!!!! He goes zingen by underneath me; idle, speed brakes - still 100 knots too fast... disappears into the dark outside our turn... rookie...

One got his share... cut him off... transfer complete... He's not moving... Waitin...

"You're done, DiamondBack".

"uh..." pause... "I show only two point five."

Trying to cheat me out of more gas... can't really blame him...

"Nice try ...see ya... you're complete..."

"No, really," the RIO pipes up. Slow to 190....

"OK!, OK! We're outta here..." Back to two twenty...

"Two, You're cleared in."

Fence, fence, stab, stab, power, push, green light, good transfer. airspeed...

Three grand... "you're done" ... no argument... he leaves... drogue stowed... done...

That was nice, quick and dirty... Doesn't always go that way... Time to go home... Hook down, first thing. Then: "Ready to copy marshall instructions".

"Texaco... You're signal buster". They're waiting on me... Recovery's almost over... Better yet... Mil power, 500 knots downhill, looking for a vector. Now, this is the way it is supposed to work; Zing on down, short turn on to final, crash it on... a little pb&j while I catch the end of the movie.... life is good... aaah...

yes... and then...

" Just a sec Texaco, we need you to stay on station. 'got another customer coming to ya."

"Who's that?"

" Clincher 421... Give im 'what you can..."

" Don't have much left... but send him up". "Tell him angels 20... things are closing up fast here ...Clobbered to 15 at least..."

Twenty's no good... ditto reports on 30 and 35... Gotta see for myself... Solid... 37.5, and my stone of a jet isn't going any higher... Sorry guy...

Mask off, settle back... They still want me to hang loose, remain on station, just in case.... in case what? Solid all the way to 40 grand... Recovery's got to be over by now... Not so tired anymore... something's up... Something that includes me... Not good.... Waitin', waitin'... waitin' for the other shoe to drop...

" Rocket, you up?" (Here comes that other shoe).

Uh oh... a voice of seniority... calling me personally... this can't be good...

" Yeah, I'm up... Go ahead..."

" We got a situation here..."

It's the airboss, and he's not callin' to chit-chat...

" Whatcha got, boss?"

" 421's "trick or treat" next pass (get aboard or divert) and Sig (our divert field) is WOXOF (zero zero) (so much for the divert option).

" What are you thinking?"

" Well, we need to get you guys rendezvoused..."

" Been trying, Boss, the weather sucks up here... solid all the way up..." and then it hits me... uh oh...

" Uh, yea... we know... We were kinda thinking... um... maybe... like we could sorta uh, get you guys together... well... under the overcast..."

Long Pause....

" Rocket? You there?"

" Uh, yea Boss... standby" He's not kidding...........Serious now... Funs over... Think...

" What you got for bases down there?"

" Three, maybe four hundred ragged. " Sheeze... Longer pause.... Wide awake...

" How much time have we got?"

" Not much." The real deal...

" Understand... I'm goin' over to CATCC... see if they can vector me down below this stuff."

" Good luck" right...

CATCC's up to speed on the plan and is right there with the vector. Mask on, volume up, don't want to miss anything... Gotta hurry... Guys way low on gas... down I go... 6000 fpm... Two thousand... break the descent... Tacan says the ships off to my left... talk to me CATCC...

"Fly heading 180, altitude your discretion..."

" Roj, one eighty the heading." ...discretion... right...

Solid at one thousand... rain now heavy... and turbulence...

Set radar altimeter to 800. Ease it down... 800, rad alt beeps, it's warning... black... beacon still illuminating cloud... crap night... Stay at 800, fly the glide slope down...

" Further left 070 intercepts final."

Left turn... cross-check the HUD... scan... Ships at seven... radar altimeter flashin' its off flag... keep it in the scan anyway... 800... stay at 800... ought to be good for the glide slope intercept... scan... scan... cross-check altimeters... stay on it... needle's coming in... turn, turn, ADI, rad alt, ADI, rad alt...don't blink... through the Hud... no ship... six and a half miles... altitude... in the clear now... think... beeep! rad alt... watch the alt, fly, fly, scan... Six miles... gear, flaps, speed check... power up... don't get slow!... AOA, Beep! get up, get it up... right a bit... on centerline now, re-correct... get up... power back on... move think, watch, don't stop... rain again and cloud... climbing... back to 800… wait for the glide slope.... in the clear... if you can call it that... needle centered... altitude steady... drifting now... stay on it... AOA checks... gotta be right on... no slack... work it... Black...   scan, watch   HUD…   ADI,   BEEEP! damn ..altitude... altitude... Glide slope commin down fast... catch it... power back... bump the nose... Start it down... Ships lights... then black... red lites inside... work work... outside black... inside red... on glide slope on centerline call the ball... 800 ft...

"Texaco's got a ball, three point two... " Wave it off Texaco".

Around I go... power up, stay on the gauges... altitude... easy climb... stay out of the bases. Clean it up... stay low... tryin' to be VMC... set rad alt at 300... left turn... scan, think, move, bring it around... let's go... come on.... CATCC in the headset...

"421, left 180 downwind..."

BEEEP! crap, scan, come on, scan! Don't dick this up!... get it around... look... keep going... rain black... inkwell night...

" CATCC! where's my guy?"

" Eight miles..."

300 feet... slow... power up... black and red... in and out... don't quit ...don't quit... bring it around... abeam now... low... way low... black... 421s gotta be 7 miles on final... think!! inkwell... Bleeker hit the water like this... don't think about it... watch that ADI... lock on it... don't pause, don't relax, don't stop...scan, scan, scan... minute or so on this heading, then bring it around.... 60 sec to make the 180... he'll cover 3 miles, want to end up just slightly behind him on final... hope he's VMC... right... he's at six and a half... gotta move. come on, bend it around 45 degrees of bank... BEEP!! Damn! watch it! scan... stay cool... vertigo just waitin' for you to lose it... stay on that ADI...keep those eyes moving...

"CATCC ? "

"Approaching 5 miles"...

I'm at 5, in a turn... He's gotta be eleven, eleven-thirty... push it up... push it up... I'll never see him outside a mile... Dirty up... gonna have to be right on him... "merged plot" the radar guys call it... midair, I call it... quick check of things inside... close enough... more important stuff right now... on final ...overshot just a bit. that's ok... re-correct... try to stay just a bit right... where is he? where is he?... BEEP! damn! where's that ship? Come on, I know you're there...

" CATCC"?

"He's at 4"

So am I... we're close... probably still above me... damn A-7... almost invisible from behind... he's on centerline... I'm a needle width right... tryin to fly inside and out... death... back and forth... in and out... black and red... black and red... I'm on centerline... look! got to be right on him... fly... fly... scan and scan ...inside... outside... look... BEEP! Crap!! Watch your altitude!! black rain... loud on the canopy... crossing the centerline... crap! get it back, get it back right... left now to stop it .... right there... hold it... two miles... in and out of the scud... jet wash! Christ! he's close... on center line! come right a hair... THERE! THERE... jeese! I can touch him!... move it in! Don't lose him! Don't lose him... suck it in! formation now... stay in tight ... don't want to lose sight. Stay on him... 10 feet ..hope he doesn't fly me into the water... stay in position... don't move, don't blink... don't stop... keep it going... hands full... want to look inside ..can't ... don't dare... eyes watering... stinging... don't blink... death grip on the stick... eyes wide... fly fly fly... relax... can't... then Paddles - calling for landing lights... you got to be kidding me.!!. Right now, I need two extra hands and 4 sets of eyeballs... a blind grab for the switch... pure luck... it's on... I'll take it... ship in my periphery... close... way close... ease ahead... put him back off my left shoulder... fly off the ship... black... soft red... where's that plane guard helo? Can't care right now... ease ahead... gear up... extend the drogue... get ready... be ready... flying back over my shoulder... BEEP!! Don't sink!... at the bow. 200 feet... watch the heading... airspeed!! Parallel the ship... come on, get aboard, get aboard... BOLTER! BOLTER! BOLTER!!! CRAP! Back on the gauges hope he's got me... 220 knots...

" You gotta tally on me 421?" ...

" I'm right on ya"...

"Roj 'hang on, coming left"... left turn... back on the gauges full time... got to get him around fast... 300 feet, be smooth... let him settle aboard... be smooth...

" Still in a left turn"... just to let him know... Approaching abeam... "rolling out" ... be smooth... downwind... plan plan... easy climb to 1000... stay ahead. of it... he's not plugged yet... he's gotta be almost out ...

"CATCC"?

" Fly heading 120 downwind leg".

"Roger keep us in tight... we don't have much left..." stay alert... ships turning... nice and easy.... 1000 feet... " How you making out Clincher?"

Nothing... he's busy... still no green light...

" CATCC, give us a turn-on at 2 miles."...

Don't screw this up!! Past abeam... raining heavy... Vis down to almost zero... Still struggling back there... I see him in the mirror... not plugged yet... dancin' in the dark... fencing with the drogue... squeak it down to 800... big pressure... be smooth... wish I could do more... CATCC...

"Come left 030, base leg".

"Commin left, nice and easy..."

CATCC- "Continue your left turn, roll out 310 for the intercept..."

Rolling out... LOC coming in fast...

" Stay with me 421 commin hard left "..

Big bank... hope he's hackin' it... rollin' out on centerline... I'm all over the panel... needles good, HUD checks. altitude, AOA, ADI... waitin' on the glide slope... rad alt... still not plugged... can't see um right now... hope he's ok, no time to look... glideslope commin down... scan... be smooth, gotta be right on... altitude, airspeed AOA, altitude, ADI, ADI, and altitude again...

no second chance... gotta do it...breathe...breathe....

"Powers 'coming back startin' down". Ship's close ...pressing it in way close...

" I'm gonna have to dump ya any sec, Clincher... Lemme know..."

CATCC- "421 and flight show you on glide slope on centerline, call the ball".

I can't! not as a flight of two!... Paddles, again... "Come on, guys, I can't take you much closer"....half a mile... "Roger, stand by" ... stalling... come on... come on... ships getting big... on and on.. gonna have to drop him ... Then another voice... OK, I'm in." YES!! YES!! YES!! Move it! Quick!! Get that transfer going!!! Switch on... come on, come on... green light! Good transfer... Paddles we're goin' around..." breathe...

Adrenaline shake... it's not over... don't stop... around the pattern... keep us out of the water... scan... scan... watch the fuel... give im' one point five... won't leave me much... one, maybe two shots at the deck... more not to think about... never over...

" Keep us wide CATCC". want to give him time to get his gas...

" 10 mile turn on, OK with you?"

"Yea that'll work..." fuel meter ticken off the gallons. 1500 ft... so much more comfortable up here... for now... eyes dry... just about done... that's it... he's done... click...

"You're complete..."

"And you sir, are a lifesaver..."

" Crown Royal, a fifth, will be payment enough..." Thunk as he pulls off the basket...

"Come up here and take the lead... I'll follow you in." He slides up alongside...

" You got the lead" ...

" Roj, I got it".

My beacon comes on ...his, goes out... formation time... and vertigo if I'm not careful... clouds thick... inflight vis down to 10 feet ...no wonder he had a time gettin' plugged... snuggled up to his green nav light... locked on... one job... stay there... three or four feet separation... cockpits' a warm nest... nav light steady... steady... don't loose him   that light is my world right now... an occasional red snapshot of his ghost form from my beacon... don't want to lose him... need to be there... just in case... green light's movin... he's turning. power up, stay with 'im... stay with im... Base leg, no doubt. should be goin' dirty soon. be ready.

" Stand by gear" "Gear now"...

A quick grab for the handle and back to the throttle... nav light bobbin around in a little 2-foot bubble... smooth it out... smooth it out... don't blink... eyes burning... don't blink...

"Standby flaps... Flaps now..."

Another blind grab... another lucky hit... nice of him to gimme the heads up... he knows it's tough sleddin' out here... A quick landing check... gear flaps hook harness antiskid dumps... on glideslope... on centerline... coming out the bottoms now... ragged... in and out... stay in position... wait...

"Three-quarters of a mile "call the ball"".

He's on his own now... I fall away to the right... give him room... pray he gets aboard... and don't fly into the water... LSO's talkin more than usual... he knows he's got to get him this time... passing the bow... clean it up... save that gas... flyin' over my shoulder, tryin' to keep sight... Ship blinks from view in a wave of zero vis... BEEEP! Damn! Back on the gauges... 300 feet... pay attention dammit!! Waiting to hear something...waiting... waiting... nothing... no bolter call... nobody looking for me... must have got him... maybe... maybe... please maybe...

I gotta ask...

" CATCC, They get that guy?"

" Affirmative, you ready to call it a night?" Relief...

" You bet, Gimme a vector, and I don't have much time".

" Come left heading 120 for downwind... and... nice job..."

" Roj, just get me around as quick as you can. I'll take a three-mile turn on".

"You got it, Texaco".

Around the pattern I go... back to the basics... scan scan... stay alert... don't relax... sweat-soaked... just another 10 minutes... not over... want to relax... can't... must not ... won't...fuel... one point two... not a lot... make this one count... Don't screw this up.

This is when it counts... Carrier flying... nothing you do out here means anything if you can't get back aboard... if you can't do it when you need to... when the pressures on... like that last guy... like now... Base leg... going dirty... landing checks by rote... speed checks with AOA... fuel 1.2... just get aboard... anticipating... the LOC coming' in fast ...left turn... big bank... watch the AOA... Thirty degrees to go localizer centering up, ought to work out just about right... roll out inside three miles... waitin' on the glideslope... check the HUD... on the centerline... 800 feet... double check the hook... for sure, don't want to forget that... glide slope coming' down... power coming back catch it just right... 700 fpm... HUD shows on and on... needles ditto... three and a half degrees on the flight path vector ought to hold it... cross-check anyway... ADI looks good ..on and on... CATCC;

" Texaco, show you on and on three-quarters of a mile call the ball".

" 424 Corsair ball one point two".

" Roger ball Corsair, deck is steady"...

Meatball, lineup, angle of attack... over and over... going just a tad high... ease the power... bump the nose... stop it... nice and easy back down... power back on... oops too much... re- correct... goin' slow... power up... in close... approaching the ramp... easing power... bump the nose... drifting left...

"Right for line up" ... yea yea I know... drop the right wing... deck coming up hard... Pop the nose up a tad... Set the hook... tense... Here it com... WHAM!!! UGH!! SLAM IT TO MIL POWER!!... BLAM!! Slammed forward... harness locks... cutting into my collar bones... screeching stop... on the four wire... yes, yes, yes...... home... in the middle of my "Ship World" again... activity all around... home... no day dreaming... move it... lites out... hook up... nose gear steering engaged... power up... power up, clear the landing area... move, move... clear ...yellow shirt slowin' me down... sorry... left turn... forward on the bow...passed to another director... turn again, slow, slower... a little left... and stop... chocks in... shut it down......thumbs up... breathe... adrenaline headache... shaking ... home... shaking... but home... breathe... just breathe...

In the cockpit and still... frozen tired... limp... head back... Eyes closed... breathe... stop... right now... Might just stay in the cockpit a while... Suns 'coming up... warm on the side of my face... pink glow on the water... gentle swaying of the ship... It's perfect right here, right now... Exhaustion never felt so good... just perfect...

Bang, Bang, Bang on the side of the fuselage... A grinning, bedraggled, glad-to-be-alive "pilot -compatriot" gawking up through the rain, a fifth of Crown offered up.

Canopy open...

" What the!?..." " Compliments of the Skipper" Yes... Like I said... perfect... Perfect indeed...

COMPLICATIONS

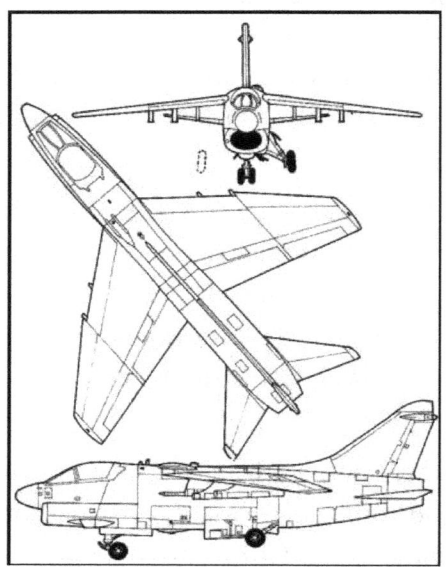

Let me say from the outset, I loved flying the A-7. More to the point, I loved the *idea* of it... single engine, single seat, one man... one machine... unparalleled mission variety, exceptional versatility, and never a dull moment. never.

I loved it for more personal reasons as well. When you've shared with an airplane the extremes of aviation, you can't help but develop a certain degree of respect and closeness to it...a special bond, if you will, not unlike that of soldiers in battle. And so it was for me and the A-7. It kept me alive through all kinds of aerial trauma and adventure, and with it, I experienced some of my most memorable moments in aviation. Of course, it was *itself* responsible for a good deal of the trauma... But, even so, you can't help but grow close to an airplane with whom you've shared those extremes... good *and* bad. And besides, memories like that are far better remembered than experienced and almost always look better in retrospect. I've often said, "It was a great airplane to *have* flown". But I digress.

The Vought A-7E Corsair II was an enormously capable airplane, much overlooked and underrated. As regards avionics, it was years ahead of its time. It came equipped with Heads Up Display, Inertial Nav, Doppler, Terrain Following Radar, Moving Map, an Automatic Carrier Landing System capable of coupled approaches all the way to touchdown (at the Carrier, no less), and an air to ground weapons delivery system that was, without question, the best there was. All this, mind you, in 1970!

It was a tough airplane, able to take the repeated abuse of Carrier takeoffs and landings, and at 42000 pounds, it has the distinction of being the heaviest single-engine airplane ever to operate routinely off the Carrier. It carried virtually every weapon in the USN's inventory (including nukes) and with an empty weight of 21000 pounds, one of the few capable of carrying its empty weight in ordinance and fuel. Oooh... And let's not forget the 6000 rounds per minute, 20 mm Gatling gun.

That said, it was not without its detractors. To be blunt about it... the engine sucked. For sure, as compared to modern jet engines, but as well, even when compared to its contemporary engines. Virtually everyone with any experience at all in the airplane has experienced their share, and then some, of engine problems, the most common of which were compressor stalls. I doubt there is an A-7 driver out there that hasn't experienced several episodes of compressor stalls. And in an airplane with just one engine, that can be very disconcerting when the second step in the emergency checklist calls for an engine shutdown and a relight attempt...right...Believe me, there is no place on or above Earth quieter than an A-7 cockpit with its engine shut down... And at night...IFR...over the ocean... It's even quieter. Then there are the turbine failures, guide vane failures, bleed valve miss-scheduling, and assorted other system failures. Like I said, it sucked.

We would joke that, "OK, maybe the A-7 had a crappy engine, but at least it only had one of 'em."

You'd think that due to its single-engine design and propensity for fairly regular malfunctions, some measure of backup or redundancy would be supplied... and you'd be wrong. We had what we had...and it wasn't much...one engine, one generator, and no battery backup... Oh, and did I mention... at night, IFR, over water? Oh sure, it *did* have a RAT (ram air turbine) that could be extended in an emergency to supply a modicum of electric or hydraulic power. Still, when the sleddin's tough, you really didn't want to *have* to rely on the RAT.

The airplane's proclivity for problems was particularly challenging at sea. Out there, there was a lot of hard flying. A lot of night, a lot of IFR, open ocean, pitching deck, and the rest. The whole "at sea" thing brought an entire other dimension to flying when it came to dealing with the various problems and malfunctions all too commonplace in the A7. Landing back aboard is challenging enough under ideal conditions. Throw in electrical or hydraulic problems, limited fuel, open ocean with no divert options, and things get very serious in a big hurry. And trust me on this, the ejection seat solves nothing. You may leave one set of problems behind, but your *real* problems have only just begun.

As professional aviators, we, of course, knew these things, but back then, we were young and indestructible, flew with reckless abandon, and as such, never gave our airplane's less- than-ideal peculiarities a second thought   most of the time, that is. Every once in a while, however, our youth's blurred vision of reality was slapped into sharp focus by events even we couldn't ignore. And so, it was to be this day.

Late summer, somewhere off the coast of Italy, in the Adriatic Sea. The Aircraft Carrier USS Eisenhower, 7 months into a 9-month deployment, 1400 Zulu. I was assigned a late afternoon post-maintenance check flight. Routine at this point in my career, I generally regarded the PMCFs as a distraction from the real missions we regularly flew. More tedious and structured and, for sure, less fun. But, stuck as we were in the narrow band of restricted airspace between Italy and Yugoslavia, we had no really significant mission assignments and were flying, more or less, just to maintain proficiency, and to...well. just to say we did it. It was, however, a chance to bag another quick daytime trap, something none of us ever turned down.

So, after suiting up, I swung by maintenance to grab a test card and take a quick look at the aircraft's logbook and mechanical history. The logs indicated that they had replaced the A7's engine and done the required ground runs, engine trim checks and adjustments. The final stage of readiness was the airborne checks, all spelled out on the test card and all required to return the aircraft to full service. Some checks were valuable, functionally important tests, and some were just BS... Like the throttle "slam and re-slam" engine fuel control checks at 41000 feet. Right... More often than not, they resulted in the aforementioned compressor stalls, engine overtemping, and requisite shutdown... Most experienced Corsair drivers just sort of skipped over that item on the test card. You see, we were fearless... not stupid.

So, with the test card in hand and the naiveté of youth, I made my way to the flight deck. A magnificent day awaited me. Calm sea state, warm temps, and good viz promised a quick up and down cycle. My airplane was just coming up the flight deck elevator, starboard side forward, set to be spotted just aft of the number 1 cat. I'd be one of the first to go. Set up in a "clean wing", low drag configuration, it was rare to fly one without the 3000-pound drop and a wing full of ordinance racks. Of course, with any of that stuff hanging on the airplane, it'd never make the 41000 feet called for on the test card, so it was only out of necessity that I got to fly it in the "slick" configuration. And although it was quite a performer in this configuration, it also meant that I'd be launching with 3000 pounds less fuel than was usual... A condition that *no* experienced Carrier aviator ever looks forward to... Ever.

Preflight, man-up, and cockpit checks were routine, and soon I was counting down the minutes to launch, bored with the waiting and anxious to get going. Thirty thousand on the weight board... should be an easy shot today at the lower weight and drag count.

Time's getting close... Movement has slowed on the flight deck. People are where they need to be, and airplanes are filling the four cats, waiting for the go. Launch imminent, I ready the cockpit for the shot. Loose gear stowed, mask on, one last check of engine and controls, and I'm set. Tomcat's the first to go, hidden partially from my view by the jet blast deflector just now coming down. Taxi director guiding me forward, launch bar down, small nose gear wiggle to engage the shuttle... Tension on the cat...brakes off, full power... all is well... Salute, and off we go.

Sshhhwwaaank!!! Off the end, rotate and turn, gear coming up, flaps and back overhead, climbing to 20 K. Ho hum...

20 K... Run through the test card, recording this temp or that pressure, N1 vs TOP, low speed, high speed...la di Dah...

Climb for the high-altitude data...

Through 40000, enjoying the view.... and... the cockpit dies... Whop... Just like that...dead...

Off flags everywhere, silence in the headset... Console lights out...Dead...

Generator's offline...Crap...

No problem.... Reset Switch... And, light and noise, it's alive again... hmmm... Think I'll skip the rest of the high

altitude stuff for now. Downhill, headed back overhead the ship, going through 400 knots, and the cockpit, again dies...takes two resets this time to get it back. Not good.

Better let somebody know before it happens ag..........CRAP!

Dead again, and this time no joy on the reset Repeated attempts to reset are fruitless, and I'm forced to deploy the RAT. Hate to have it come to that, but... here goes... pull it... Comes out with a clunk, spins up and dies... Recycle No good... Try another generator reset.... dead...sigh...OK... no problem...no generator, no RAT.   Complete electrical failure. Let's see. We've studied this. Read the book. It's on the checklist. Sure...no problem...Sure...

Not Quite

The checklist is effectively worthless. It's basically there to list all the things you don't have, leaving it up to you to discover the painful truth of how it'll play out in the real world.

Thanks...

OK, it is a problem... in fact, a big problem as I was about to learn. It's one thing to read through the procedures and memorize the checklists...to recite the list of inop things you suddenly wish you had... It is quite another thing to *deal* with the things you don't have...in an environment that's, shall we say, less than hospitable.

Thankfully, much of what could have caused a real disaster

for me is not a factor. To wit: The weather is good, it's daylight VFR, and the engine, the reason I'm even *here*, seems to be behaving itself.

"First things first... Hook down.... Out here...that's always" the first step. For sure don't want to forget that. Second, extend the refueling probe... ooops...it's on the list, inop.

Next... Time. How long do I have to work on this problem? Daylight is not an issue, so time reduces to fuel.

Fuel...Fuel

...Ut oh...

Thinking back on my ground school and remembering what I can of the fuel system, I'm left with an empty feeling in the pit of my stomach. I run through the system in my head twice before resigning myself to the painful truth.

The fuel transfer and feed system continuously and automatically cycles between wing fuel transfer and fuselage fuel transfer modes. With an electrical failure, the transfer cycle *stays where it last was*. This means that the transfer *could* be stuck in the fuselage mode where *as little as 500 pounds could be left available!!!* I probably have close to 8000 pounds on board but possibly only 500 usable! Damn and damn. 500 pounds! That's 15 minutes! And that's clean! In the landing configuration, that's maybe once around the pattern!

Course, it may be stuck in the wing cycle, which will give me more time, but I have no way of knowing that and am not about to assume it. Even if I knew it were, I've got no fuel gauges! I could make a pretty good guess, but I could never know exactly how much fuel I had remaining. This all means, among other things, that a divert is out of the question...it's back aboard or. well, at least the seat will work.

I try not to think about that.

So... slow it down....max conserve ... Save what little gas you might have, head for the ship, and tell them what's up... They'll need to know...

Yes, tell them what's up...

Crap... no radios.... The dreaded list of things you don't have rears its ugly head.... again...I scramble to fish the PRC90 emergency radio out of my survival vest...the airplane's all over the sky (no autopilot), and every time I let go of the stick, the airplane wants to do an outside loop (no trim). Finally, able to wrestle it free, I wriggle the earpiece under the helmet and into my ear and transmit...

"Mayday, Mayday, Clincher 24 transmitting on guard.

Anybody up?"

Nothing...

Transmit again.... nothing again... not surprised... the PRC 90 is a notorious POS. I don't waste time dickin' with it... More pressing matters. And time is running out...

Slowed down around 200, max endurance, it takes almost three hands to hold the nose up (remember, the trim quit at 400 knots).

I've got to let someone know... can't just show up behind the ship and expect a clear deck. Plus, I'll be no flap and overweight. Ironic that with as little as 500 pounds of fuel available to me, I'm overweight for landing *because* of fuel. The trapped wing fuel is dead weight, and without fuel dumps available, I'm stuck bringing it back aboard. Overweight and no flaps have me coming aboard at 180 knots or so, something the ship will damn sure need to know... something I absolutely *need* them to know. The maximum engaging speed for the arresting gear is 145 knots in the A-7. Any

closure speed higher, and I risk either yanking the hook off and subsequent ejection, or, worse yet, snapping the arresting cable.

A snapped cable is nor a pretty sight and invariably does hellish damage to anything and anyone that gets in its two- inch-thick steel cable whip-cracking way.

My necessarily high approach speed will require the ship to put at least 35 knots of wind across the deck...not easily done in most ships but, fortunately, the Ike is nuclear-powered and can easily accelerate to put whatever wind across the deck may be required. But they need to *know* they have to. Right now, though, from what I can see from the ship's wake, they're making maybe 8 knots... minimum for steerage. That is not at all acceptable, not something I'm even willing to attempt.

Plus, the ship will need time to clear the landing area, notify the LSOs, and make a "ready deck". That'll take time, and time is one thing I may not have a lot of. I've got to tell someone... And I've got to do it quickly. Then it hits me...Of course! The Tanker! There's always a tanker on station...probably in a port orbit in the mid-teens somewhere. I'm overhead the ship descending through 20 when I spot the tanker, a KA6 Intruder, across the circle from me, refueling a couple of Tomcats. Cutting across the circle, I race to join, and just as quickly, overshoot with 50 knots of overtake (no speed brakes). I eventually gather myself and slide over close aboard his right side and, with hand signals, indicate to the BN in the right seat my type of emergency and status. He returns a thumbs up and appears to understand, but I'd feel a lot better if it were a KA7 (A7 tanker) up here instead, somebody who for sure understands what an electrical failure means in *this* airplane.

Still, if he's sharp, he'll pass the word to our Squadron rep and let him fill the Air Boss in with all the nasty details.

The BN pats his shoulder, indicating I should stay on his wing... He'll lead me in. Sorry, but I can't count on him understanding the time-critical nature of what I'm dealing with or the specifics of my no-flap configuration... I tap my watch and peel off to set up for landing on my own and hope the Tanker has passed the word on. I try, without success, a couple more generator resets as I maneuver myself for my approach. Still no luck. Rolling out two miles aft of the ship and lined up, I can see the deck still being "respotted" in what is called an "emergency pull forward". I pray they understand the urgency of my predicament but at the same time, understand that things can only move so fast with a deck full of airplanes.

Aircraft are still fouling the deck at a mile and a half, but I continue on in hopeful anticipation. At a mile and a quarter, I blow the gear down, holding it to the very end, trying to save fuel till the last possible minute. I'm committed ... the gear is down to stay... no retraction possible... no refueling possible...And my fuel is now, very fast waning. I've got maybe 10 minutes... once around the pattern.

Then, more from the "things you don't have " list. The angle of attack indexers, critical to landing aboard, are gone... HUD - gone... auto throttles - gone... No flaps has me flying close to 180 knots on final, and the out-of-trim condition is at its worst... Approaching a mile, the lens and meatball are still off. They'll stay off until the deck is clear and the LSO is on station. Three-quarters of a mile, normal "ball call" distance...still no lens.

The ship is turning, looking for the wind but still appears to still be making minimum headway. Damn and damn. Half a mile, and I can't press it any further... Push it up and go around... Staying low as I pass the island, I give the Air Boss a good look at my no-flap configuration and hope our Squadron rep has gotten the word to him about my predicament, and it's time-dependent consequences. I've got maybe one more pass before I'm finished. I bend the airplane around sharply, staying close aboard.... anxious to see how close to ready the deck is. It looks like good news... the landing area appears clear, the last of the "pull forward" is complete. Even more beautiful to me is the sight of massive white water churning in the wake just aft of the ship. The Boss has got it! The ship is pouring on the coals, accelerating to give me my life-saving wind across the deck. Now it's up to me... I've got one shot at this. Rolling through the ninety-degree position, I pick up the lens and meatball. The LSO gives me a shot of green lights just to let me know he's there and ready. Rolling out in the "groove", on the glideslope, I'm doing 180 despite what feels like a grotesquely nose-high attitude. I start to go a little high in close, bump the nose, and reset the attitude crossing the ramp and come down hard on the three wire. The nose rotates down hard as I mash the throttle to full, just in case. For a split second, I worry that I've hook skipped and am going around, destined to flame out halfway around the pattern. Then, WWWRRRAAAG, the four wire's sudden deceleration slams me forward into my shoulder harness, leaving my fate now solidly in the hands of the ship's below-deck system of cables and capstans, doing its hydraulic best to stop me on the deck remaining. I run the wire out way down the deck, almost to full extension, cringing in frightened anticipation, waiting for a cable snap or some ancillary disaster to send me over the side and to my watery demise...

Luck is with me this day, and I come to rest, safely held stationary despite the still military power emanating from my engine.

Back to reality.................throttle idle, hook up, engage nose gear steering...oops forgot   No nose gear steering. Another from the "things you don't have list"... My pantomimed "no nose gear steering" hand signals go unheeded, and so I sit, holding the brakes, hoping sooner or later, the guys on deck will figure out what I'm waiting for. For several minutes the deck hands mill about anxiously, annoyed at my apparent disregard for deck protocol and efficiency, cussing, I'm certain, at my thoughtless intrusion into their otherwise perfectly choreographed re-spot. But eventually, the word gets down to them that I'll need a tow. They move quickly to flag down a tractor and get me out of their hair and securely chained down and chocked. And just like that, it's over.

It's amazing to me how quickly things go back to normal. I'm out of the way and put away. The re-spot continues as if nothing out of the ordinary has happened—just another day. I guess maybe out here, the extraordinary *is* the norm, and everyday occurrences are *necessarily* exceptional. Even still, things could have easily gone so much worse... a couple of knots faster on the approach, a few pounds heavier, a few more seconds.... anyone of those minute differences could have spelled disaster for me and too many on deck. In cases like these, you'd have to say luck played an important, if not primary, role. I did what I could, the ship did what it could, and the rest was up to chance.

I climb down from the jet and meet, head on the Squadron Maintenance Chief and several of his guys waiting anxiously to talk. I explained how the generator crapped out, resets, no good...the PRC 90, no good...and how the RAT, my last line of defense, let me down as well...

"Yea, Yea... Lieutenant, but how'd the engine run?" "Oh, The engine? .... It worked just fine..."

And with that, they turned and headed back below decks and to their waiting coffees.

Reflecting back on the flight, I'm humbled... even embarrassed to have learned such an important lesson this late in my career. The idea of thinking through *every* consequence of *any* particular emergency in precise enough detail to cover every contingency and at the same time, *keeping it "real-time accurate" requires* far more imagination and far more preparation than I had anticipated. Perhaps more than is even possible when so much is dependent on the ever-developing complexities that, too often, accompany even the simplest of emergencies

VERTIGO

It was one of the most wretched nights I've ever had the distinct displeasure of flying through. Rain, fog, wind, low scud...and black. No moon...no stars...over ocean...down low... inky, stinky, nothing, black. At least we didn't have to land back aboard the ship...

I was number four in a flight of four A7s, and we were part of a large Alpha Strike exercise incorporating various fighter, attack, and support elements from our Air Wing. We were staging out of Rosy Roads NAS, Puerto Rico in a series of exercises designed to check our readiness for our planned upcoming Mediterranean deployment aboard the USS Eisenhower. On paper, our flight's role in tonight's mission looked simple enough, even given the miserable weather. Largely an exercise in timing, we were simulating a four-plane low-level strike on an enemy battle group stationed 300 miles out into the Atlantic. We were scheduled to be the second attack element on scene at the target, with 60 seconds between subsequent arrivals.... So, the timing had to be just right... There was no room for either early or late target arrival. We'd been given a time, synched our watches and were assigned a low-level run-in heading that should keep us clear of other strike elements on different run-in headings and different " times on target".

The skipper was leading our flight and had the responsibility of delivering us to the station, plus or minus 5 seconds. The rest of us just had to hang on, fly formation, and drop our ordinance when the skipper dropped his... sounded simple enough. But, as I was about to find out, things don't always turn out the way you would like them to turn out.

I'm not sure how I ended up number 4. I had two cruises under my belt, more experience than 2 or 3, but, alas, they were both senior to me and so it was with me that they'd be playing "crack the whip".

The plan was to take off as two flights of two, and join as four on top of the overcast, en route to our initial fix, point Alpha. From there, joined as four, we would turn 90 left, establish ourselves on our run-in heading and descend to 200 feet, and accelerate to 350 knots - our pre-briefed run-in altitude and speed. From there, we would drop our high drag ordinance and exit on the same run-in heading we used inbound. This was really plain vanilla for us at this point, seasoned as we were.

Walking out to the planes, our usual ribald banter and boyish horseplay were conspicuously absent. It was late, the weather sucked, we were tired, and none of us wanted to be there. But there we were, and so it's best now to concentrate and get it over with without busting our asses.

The wind was kicking up as I settled into my darkened cockpit. The stormy night and the sideways drizzle it inspired slapped annoyingly at my face as if daring me to take it on, openly mocking my brazen disregard for Mother Nature's obvious superiority.

Not so silently cussing the night, I pulled the canopy closed, and now, alone and dripping in the darkness, I mechanically went about my tasks of readiness, more than a little annoyed at how things were shaping up.

I'm finally up and running, as are lead and two. Number three, my section lead, is having some kind of Nav problem and had to restart his inertial alignment. So at least another 13 minutes before he'd be ready. The Skipper is keeping us together, at least for now, figuring we'll make the time up airborne en route to point

Alpha.

And so, we sit. Time passes, rain falls, and the night wears on. I'm miserable. The "magic" of this mission is gone, for me at least, and our timing is becoming increasingly problematic.

Our carefully briefed plan is falling apart by the minute. It's not my place to say anything, but I'm getting more and more antsy and just want somebody to say something about anything. I'm embarrassed to find myself silently wishing fuel were an issue, a convenient and reasonable excuse to scrub the whole launch and retire to the O'Club and a beer.

At long last, and despite my otherwise wishes, three is up and ready. We taxi as four to the approach end of the runway spraying through puddles of standing water while I, out of habit, start wondering about the runway's condition and its effect on our takeoff performance; particularly me, as number 4, having to splash through the kicked up, low visibility mess made by the three aircraft before me…

On the runway, our engine checks are done, and com checks are complete. I watch as the lead and two roll as one toward the far end of the runway. I lose sight of both of them early in the takeoff roll, obscured as they were by kicked up waterspray, vapor, and the night.

Ten seconds after they roll, we roll. As a section, three and I slowly accelerate through the muck left behind by the first section. Visibility down the runway is terrible, 1/4 mile or so, and I pray silently that my lead can keep us on the runway at least long enough to get to flying speed. As for me, I only need 15 feet or so to see my lead, so on we go.

Rotation comes and we two lift off as one. Gear and flaps up and blam! into the clag, we plunge.

In flight, visibility in the clouds is down to 20 feet or so, and I find myself flying formation on the only thing I can see... my lead's green wingtip navigation light.

Turbulence is hammering away at the two of us as I struggle, not so gamely to keep the green navigation lite under some semblance of control.

At long last, we break out on top, 20,000 feet, under a moonless star-filled night. It's as smooth as silk, and I loosen my death grip on the stick and fall back, relaxing to allow my lead some room to maneuver us into position for rendezvous with the lead and # 2.

We slide aboard in a loose echelon and turn quickly to head toward point Alpha. We are running late, and the skipper has pushed us up to 300 knots in the descent. Back in the clouds and descending to our predetermined "run in"

altitude, the turbulence is at its worst.

I'm all over the sky, trying to follow 3 as he tries his best to hang on to 2. It's crack the whip at its finest, and with the inflight visibility so low, I can't even see the lead or two.

So, I'm relegated to hang on as best I can, pitching wildly in a not-so-successful attempt to stay in some kind of reasonable position on number 3's *very* out-of-control green nav light...

The punishing descent continues. The radar altimeter warning announces our arrival at 1000 feet, and we slow our rate of descent while still being battered by the fists of turbulence and the occasional sheet of zero visibility rain.

Finally, we break out of the clag. Five hundred feet and still on course for point Alpha, we are flying a loose echelon formation when the skipper powers up to the preplanned run- in speed of 350 knots.

We hit point Alpha and begin our 90-degree turn to the run-in heading while descending to 200 feet. The timing seems about right from the little I can glean from my half- second glances back inside the cockpit. I feel as if I'm all over the sky trying to fly off of three.

The whip cracking is at its worst, or, more likely, I'm just overly tired, frustrated, and pissed off and my airmanship reflects it all too accurately.

The turn to the run-in course is taking forever. Something is wrong. It's just ninety degrees, for Christ's sake! It feels as if we have done a complete 360. Certainly, the skipper wouldn't be delaying our run-in as late as we are. After the second 360, I couldn't take it anymore. Something was *very* wrong, and no one seems to have realized it. So, I take a quick glance inside to see why we are still in the turn. The attitude gyro showed wings level??!! Wha?? Wings *level*??!! I looked back outside, and I swear, just that quick, the entire formation was upside down!! Yes… Upside down!! At 200 feet and 350 knots!! The picture before me could not have been more real. It was dangerously surreal. I knew immediately that it was the devil vertigo that was after me. And it took every ounce of my will power to fight the beast I knew it could be. I knew intellectually what it was but still could not overcome the intense feeling falsely foisted upon me. So powerful a sensation that I could literally feel myself coming out of the seat as if actually inverted ! I shook my head and yelled out loud, trying to shake myself from this death trap in the making. I looked back at the standby attitude gyro to confirm our straight and level status and tried desperately to force its elusive truth into my dangerously altered vestibular condition. I knew in that moment how so many pilots were lost at sea. And how easy death came to some. I couldn't do it anymore. The tendency to roll upright and pull was almost overpowering. I would be dead in seconds. And no one would even know it until the run was over.

I am literally shaking with a life-or-death decision...I just couldn't trust myself to keep it together any longer. I knew I had to do something... something not easy... something drastic. And so, swallowing my pride...

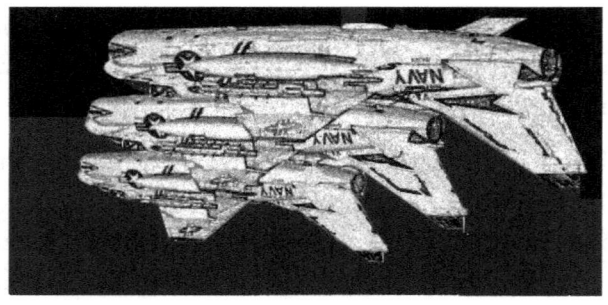

"Skipper, number 4 has got vertigo pretty bad".

Those may well have been my last words were it not for the skipper's immediate response:

"Hang in there, stay with us. We're climbing", and immediately broke off the run and started a gentle climb. Bless you, Rich Curtis. A mere 400 feet later, the world reset itself, and things were as if they had never happened. Perfectly normal equilibrium with no lingering aftereffects; Balance restored.

My emotions, however, were overloaded... I was relieved, amazed, humbled, and physically drained... Never before had I felt the effects of vertigo so dangerously expressed and so nearly deadly.

The flight back to base was uncharacteristically quiet and, thankfully, uneventful. Knowing my squadron mates as I did, I was prepared for the mountain of grief that'd be dumped on me once on the ground.

As it happened, very little ribbing took place. I suspect because they had all, at one time or another, been through a similar situation, their "night in the barrel," as is said. We have all been there and know how elusive that firm grasp on reality can sometimes be. How overwhelming things can get. I was lucky. I can only imagine how many others weren't as lucky and didn't make it back.

I learned several important lessons that night. About the unseen dangers lurking about, patiently waiting to strike the unsuspecting, about forces that can so completely overtake one's sense of what is real, and the lifesaving value of putting aside one's ego and admitting one's own weakness.

THE MYSTERIOUS ISLAND

There exists on this planet a place of almost unimaginable strangeness. It is as bizarre a place as you will ever think of, as unlikely as you can comprehend, and then some—a land that is so incredibly alien that its mere existence on Earth seems a defiance of Mother Nature herself, an aberration of life as we know it... a true oddity of the first order. From its fantastic, other-world landscape to its monster-like inhabitants, it's almost inconceivable any human can survive for more than minutes amidst its treacherous environs. But survive, they do. This is the true story of their world...

Theirs is a diminutive, island-like land, an isolated speck of existence, insignificant in a vast ocean. No ordinary island is like this, oh no, for it is truly an island like no other. There are no beaches, no hotels, and no palms under which to lounge or mai tais by the pool. In short, it is about as anti-tourist as anyplace might be. And for good reason.

Its land surface is virtually featureless, a flat as a fritter slab of rocklike hardness whose entire perimeter consists of sheer cliff walls - a deadly drop off into the ocean's grip for any man or beast unlucky enough to misstep or, as you shall see, succumb to the land's many impediments to survival.

The surface itself is covered with a thin layer of viscous residue slime that makes travel a slip-and-slide affair under all but the most ideal conditions. Unfortunately, rarely do there exist ideal conditions in this land. The wind howls most days at gale force, steady and unrelenting, threatening to topple any, save the most surefooted of individuals. At night, without a moon, it is as dark and as foreboding as any uncivilized wasteland. Only a dim, soft glow of light emanating from somewhere high up in the land's sole mountain peak provides any respite from the all-enveloping darkness. Even still, movement about the land is treacherous and safe passage is far from guaranteed. The careless don't last long here.

And then... there are the Monsters...

These are not the Monsters of legend, oh no, for they are all too real... all too deadly. True beasts they are... mindless, twenty-ton behemoths... brainless slugs of such ferocity, of such vile and unpredictable behavior that their presence alone makes survival on the island a virtual 24-hour-a-day battle just to stay alive.

Every day and every night, the island abounds with these wretched creatures, each moving about haphazardly with an apparent single-minded goal... to devour anything and everything in their path. Theirs is a hunger that is never satisfied, never enough. They'll eat anything, at any time, and do it with savage disregard for any and all life. Discriminating eaters, they surely are not. Anything goes... debris and detritus, waste or resource... and of course, people. It's as though they have evolved through time for the sole purpose of eating and to that end, have developed their physical systems to serve that singular purpose. So great is their need for sustenance that during their waking hours, they seek to ingest their meals almost continuously and inhale with such gulping force that anything within twenty feet of the Beast's gaping maw is instantly whooshed off the ground and thrown into the brute's ample gullet. More than a few careless individuals have been whisked clean off their feet and tossed headfirst into the beasts waiting mouth and slathering teeth. And talk about teeth!! ...twenty rows of razor-sharp grinding masticators that can turn a human being to liquid in seconds, expelling the unrecognizable amalgam from its hind quarters with a force that will easily bowl over anyone or anything within twenty feet of the beast's rear end. To the wandering unaware, the Beast's flatulent expulsion, more often than not, results in the victim's rapid head-over-heels cartwheel over the edge of the island's natural precipice and into the ocean void to be lost forever. This is not a land for the unaware.

The creatures roam freely, haphazardly, and with apparent disregard for anything save their insatiable drive for sustenance. They brazenly announce their presence with a hellish roar, a cacophony of frequencies reverberating throughout the land that continues unabated for as long as they are awake, a roar whose range extends from earsplitting ultrasonics to a nauseating base pounding that has driven more than one man deaf from exposure, sick to his stomach and running for cover.

They are the undisputed masters of the land and move about with the arrogant confidence of superiority, safe in the knowledge that nothing alive can touch them. They are the most cunning, sly, deceiving, skulking cheaters. Ponderously slow most of the time, they can, in a moment's notice and with no warning, whatever, pivot on one foot, swinging that twenty-foot death cone of vacuum across in front of them scavenging up everything in its path with devastating results for those caught off guard. And then, just as quickly, they can take off running at a clip that would turn a cheetah green with envy. At full stride, the Beasts can reach speeds far greater than any other animal on Earth, and no one can escape their microsecond acceleration. They are uncatchable and unavoidable. Woe betides anyone who wanders unwittingly into their path.

And so, if you will, try and imagine... the black of night, wind howling at gale force, treacherous footing every step of the way, slipping and sliding, head splitting thunderous shrieking, an unpredictable turning, pivoting, racing starving Beast every thirty feet and nowhere to hide, no weapons to bear. Why would anyone attempt survival under these conditions? Why indeed.

And so, there you have it; and unlikely story of an unlikely land... or is it? The fact is, these and other dangers are confronted by hundreds of individuals every day on these strange islands all over the world. Islands with names like Lincoln, Stennis and Enterprise... Aircraft Carriers on whose flight decks these not- so-strange happenings are an everyday occurrence, a routine battle fought and won on a daily basis by the brave men and women of the United States Navy.

NIKKI'S FLIGHT

They were just two in the crowd, and it was them that I noticed... a young mother and her daughter, I presumed, standing side by side, looking out over the ramp of airplanes from the wooden observation deck at the St. Augustine Airport. They were strangers to the airport, almost certainly, but unlike the other spectators, they seemed less interested in the goings on, very obviously distracted, as if they were just going through the motions of having fun. Their faces were tired and wan, almost old-looking—starkly contrasting to their lithe physiques and otherwise obvious youth. Nevertheless, the young woman was trying her best to make excitement out of the scene for her little girl, but her put-on smile was forced... and sad.

The little girl, six, maybe seven years old, was sullen and withdrawn. She stood quietly by with her head tilted to rest lightly against her mom's hip while she watched with uncommitted interest... alone in her mind, it seemed... distant.

Driving by, I tossed a quick wave to the little girl. She was oblivious, staring blankly in my direction while playing lazy circles in her long blond hair with a tiny finger.

I continued by and on to the hangar, not really anxious to work on the Cub but determined at least to get the oil changed before quitting. I worked absently for a while, forgetting twice how many quarts I had added, and so decided that maybe I should take a break for lunch.

On the way out, I was driving by the terminal when I saw them again, the little girl walking slowly, tears rolling down her cheeks, sobbing gently with her mom bent alongside in helpless despair.

"Come on, sweetie", I heard her say, gently pulling her daughter to her side. "We'll go to McDonalds for lunch, OK?... Would you like that?"

Her voice shook, anxious for her little girl to smile.

My heart sank as I drove away. I could see them in the mirror: Two people alone, shuffling slowly toward a beat-up old blue Volkswagen.

After lunch, I drove to the bank. I was bothered by the thought of them. Try as I might, I just couldn't get them off my mind. Their lives were in turmoil, at least for the moment, and I wondered what trauma had brought them to this point in their lives. I didn't know and would most likely never know, but the scene, so poignant, so real, just wouldn't leave me alone.

I needed to fly, to clear my head. The Cub was eager to help as always, and soon I was relaxing 1000 feet over the beach in the sea breeze smooth afternoon. Twenty minutes was all I needed—two landings to top it off and then back to the hanger I taxied.

I had just rounded the corner of the maintenance shop when, like an unfinished story, I saw them....

They were standing together, side by side, in their matching outfits, mom's firm grip keeping her little one safe on the ramp of unfamiliar territory. They watched quietly and with plain stares, the little girl still clutching her "Happy Meal", as I taxied by and parked four doors down in front of my open hanger. I climbed out, lifted the tail and managed the airplane into its spot without too much difficulty, and headed to the terminal for a Coke.

I would have stopped to talk to them, I wanted to, but my casual intrusion into their obvious melodrama just didn't seem right. I purposely passed maybe 50 feet away when out of the corner of my eye, I noticed the young woman approaching. She was hesitant, awkward and uncomfortable... This was not easy for her.

"Excuse me", her voice shuddered, "Do you know if anyone gives airplane rides here?"

" Sure ", I said, trying my best to put her at ease. "Would that be for you or the little punkin' over there?"

" Oh, not for me... it would be for Nicole ".

Nicole stood by patiently, under clear orders, not to wander off while we walked over. I knelt down to her.

" Hey Nicole, your mom says you might want to go flyin'... that right?"

She hesitated only briefly, then nodded a head down affirmative, shuffling her feet in classic little girl fashion, her big blue eyes lowered, studying a lone pebble at her feet.

" Ok, good then, come on over to the hangar and help me get the airplane ready".

Nicole watched with apparent apathy as I eased the Cub out of the hangar and into the sunlight. If she was eager to fly, I sure couldn't't tell.

After a quick preflight, I lifted her gently into the front seat while her mom stood silently by, unsure of just what to do or how to feel.

I hand-propped the Cub from behind, then reached across Nicole to work the throttle to a slow idle. I double-checked her seat belt and watched her eyes narrow as she studied the dials that had come alive in front of her. She was more occupied now, and I felt better for her.

Climbing quickly into the back seat, I mouthed what I hoped was a reassuring "don't worry" to her mom, still standing by the right wing.

We taxied lazily to the runway, did our checks, and positioned ourselves on to the centerline.

" You all set, Nicole?"

Again, she nodded in affirmative.

" Ok, here we go!"

With that, the power came up, and the little Cub floated forward. We bounced into the air 600 feet later and turned softly up and away from the field.

Almost immediately, I could see a change in Nicole. She shifted herself to sit up tall, suddenly more curious. Grabbing the cabane, she pulled herself up to look over the nose, then turned around to see the tail through the Cub's open door. There was excitement building in her, I could see it in her eyes. The color returned to her cheeks as, bit by bit, the little girl's exuberance returned to her face.

We climbed steadily back overhead the field, banking

steeper and steeper toward the Cub's open-door side. I watched her closely as the G's increased. Nicole looked down, unafraid and at ease - almost giddy from the dizziness of the maneuver. Her eyes were shining now, and she was alive with her newfound excitement. I could almost hear her little heart racing.

Then in a second, her face turned serious... With her eyes narrowed, she studied the ground. She spotted her mom and pointed, and then laughed a quick squeal when the 70-mph wind pushed at her arm. She turned to me, laughed, then pushed at the air again just for fun.

Round and round, we turned, spiraling up over the airport. Nicole leaned into the turns, openly excited now, her golden hair like wildfire in the open-door breeze. She was at the same time captivated and captivating, waving hugely to her mom on the ground, laughing freely when the steep turn G's got heavy.

She seemed natural in the air, so we flew some wingovers—big, tall ones—floating slowly through the weightless arc at the top. She turned left, then right, and then left again as if to capture the event from every angle, recording for later, every second of every moment. Then we flew over the beach, down low to look for dolphins, rocking our wings and waving big hellos to the occasional sunbather passing silently beneath our wheels.

So occupied was she with her new adventure I hardly think she noticed when we throttled back to land on the grass. She turned back to me, just briefly, as if to question the move, then nodded understanding when I leaned out and pointed to the grass runway just below our nose. Her eyes took on that curious look again as she watched the tall weeds reach up for the tires. With her left hand on the cabane, she leaned out with her right, feeling the air as it slowed.

We plopped into the grass and rolled to a quiet stop in the openness of the grassy field. Only the afternoon's soft breeze and the Cub's gentle idling disturbed the peaceful serenity of the moment. Nicole was quiet now and still. With a distant, faraway look in her eyes, she stared down at the Cub's tire. A stray wind blew her hair softly across her face hiding the welling in her eyes. With little effect, she sat motionless, her left hand still on the cabane, her right now limp on the fabric of the Cub's lower door.

Then, in absent monotone and to no one, I heard her whisper... "Poor mommy" ... The words hung in the air while Nicole stared unblinking as if waiting for them to settle into the grass. I stared at her profile, frozen in the moment, afraid to do or say anything for fear of upsetting whatever tender balance of little girl emotion existed in her.

Then, she looked up, and just like that, she was her little girl self again, anxious to find her mom and tell her all about her new adventure. I tapped her on the shoulder and pointed. There she was, waiting nervously alongside the taxiway, still carrying Nicole's Happy Meal. Nicole waved wildly while we bumped our way across the grass toward the hanger. Her mom caught us on the run and then jogged easily alongside, half smiling, half crying for the joy her little girl had obviously found. "I love you, Nikki". I could see her say, "I love you too, Mommy," she giggled back.

Back at the hanger, Nicole had her seat belt undone almost before I could shut down, and only a firm grip on her shoulder kept her from jumping out before the propeller stopped.

Once released, she bounded from the plane, leaping off the tire, arms motioning, hair flying, jumping from thought to thought in mid-sentence, her mom still 20 feet away. Her pent-up energy was released. She was alive again! Grabbing her mom's hand, she ran, skipped, and jumped her way across the ramp, letting go again and again when only a two-handed explanation of her flight would do.

Nikki's mom, dragged along by this sudden new ball of energy, turned to me over her shoulder, purse in hand, her eyes questioning. She looked as if the weight of ten worlds had been lifted from her shoulders. Her wind-tasseled hair did little to hide the tears of happiness flowing from her eyes, and at that moment, I couldn't't think of a more satisfying payment. I waved a "forget about it" sort of wave and sat down on the tire to watch them dance out of sight.

For a long time, I sat and thought about them, about their life together and about who would carry who through the coming years; about the impact a lazy afternoon at the airport could have on a person, and if the Cub would ever realize what an important role it played in two people's lives.

I pushed the airplane into the hanger, chocked its tires, and patted its nose. It was a happy Cub, and I was glad again that we two had found each other. As I closed the hanger doors, I took one last look at the Cub sitting there in the dark and thought: How is it, little Cub... How is it you can do these things... these things that defy understanding... creating life where none existed, a beginning from an end, and a smile on a sad little girl's face...

Epilogue

About a year later, a letter arrived at the St. Augustine Airport addressed to "The man with the red, white and blue Cub plane". It was postmarked Fairbanks, Alaska, and was from Meghan, Nikki's mom. It read:

Dear Sir,

    I'm sorry I never got your name, so I hope this letter finds its way to you. I want to let you know what a difference you made in my and Nikki's life and to thank you for your generosity and thoughtfulness. Nikki's joy that day was life-altering for her and a much-needed wake-up call for me. We found new strength in each other, the strength we needed to move on. We are living in Fairbanks, Alaska now, and we love it. I'm teaching at the local elementary school, and Nikki is happier than I've seen her in a long time. We talk often of her flight with you. She's at her happiest talking about it, although I confess to being unable to answer all her airplane questions, of which she has many. She has made friends with some of the bush pilots at the local airstrip, where, at her insistence, we spend most of our Saturday afternoons.

You changed our lives. Thank you. Sincerely, Meghan P.S. Oh, and of course, Nikki wants me to get her flying lessons for Christmas. Enclosed was a picture of the two of them, sitting on the open tailgate of their pickup truck, happy as happy can be, Nikki, resplendent in her too large flying jacket and Meghan in matching attire, both clearly enjoying their newfound life and happiness together.

FULTON

The room full of people stared uncomfortably at the developing situation in the flight school lobby while the less than tactful chief pilot sputtered clumsily, trying to resolve his awkward predicament.

"I'm sorry, sir, but um...we can't ...uh...I mean it's going to be ...um.... well...we don't have the.... uh...It's just that you're well...just...well, you're too...you know..."

" Yes...I know......Never mind..."

And with that, the big man in the wheelchair turned and motored his way toward the door. Three people jumped to get the door, a little too anxious to mollify the young man's embarrassment, and instantly felt ashamed for it.

"I got it", he said simply, and with his one good arm, pushed open the door while elbowing the go-forward lever of his motorized chair.

I couldn't believe what I had just witnessed.

"Dennis! What the hell was that?!" I asked, angry at the thoughtless manner in which he dealt with the young man.

"Whaddaya mean?! He wants to go for a ride... Look at him, he's 350 pounds if he's an ounce! He'd never fit! And if he did, we'd never get off the ground... Did you *see* him?"

"Yea, I *did* see him, Dennis. I saw him managing himself into his van, *by himself*, which he no doubt drove here, *by himself*... And I saw him come in here, *knowing* that, more than likely, he'd get an embarrassing turn down... But he did it anyway... Do you think *you'd* have the guts to do that yourself? "

I was angry and had to leave before I said something I'd

really regret. I ran out to the parking lot and caught up with the young man just as he was maneuvering himself into the driver's position of his van.

I tapped on the window...you?"

"Excuse me... you came here for an airplane ride, didn't "Well, yea..."

"I'll tell you what, if you'll work with me, we'll try and get it done...what do you say?"

" Sure, if you think..."

"I don't think... I know... You wanna go flying... We're gonna take you flying."

I stood by while he maneuvered his way to the back of his van and onto the lift. He lowered himself down, stowed the hydraulic lift, closed and locked up his van. He rotated his chair to face me and, extending his left hand said simply, " Fulton".

Taking his left hand in mine...., "Fulton?... Carl...pleased to meet you..."

I knelt down to him while we talked candidly about his physical limitations...what he could and couldn't do, and what he could do with a little help. I was impressed with how capable he was despite his obvious physical handicap and was immediately embarrassed at my stereotypical prejudgment.

He couldn't stand; his legs had long ago atrophied, and while he had movement in his right arm, he admitted to having no strength there. No problem...I had an idea. Fulton followed me up the ramp and into the FBO, gawking wide-eyed when he noticed the colorful quarter-scale models hanging from the ceiling. He spun round and round in his chair, looking all of 8 years old...an enthusiast of the first order.

I poked my head into Jim Moser's office (the FBO owner)

... "Hey Jim, I'm going to borrow the 182 for a while"... It wasn't a question.

I grabbed the keys and, heading out the door, asked Scotty, the lineman, to round up some of the other "line" guys, a toolbox, and meet me out at Jim's 182.

Fulton followed me out to the airplane and around it as I did my preflight checks, stopping me occasionally to ask this or that about the airplane, what I was checking for, and assorted other questions. I stopped at the passenger side door while Fulton looked askance at the prospect of fitting into the seat.

"Not to worry, Fulton, we got it covered."

It took us about 5 minutes to completely remove the seat, leaving more than ample floor space for Fulton to sit. We stole a couple of blankets from the back office and padded the floor where the chair rails ran. Not exactly the most legal setup, but I was bound and determined to take Fulton flying, and the heck with the FARs.

" We got no seatbelt Fulton, but if you're OK with it, I'm OK."

"I'm good". But I could see skepticism about our next issue in his eyes.

The five of us stared stupidly at each other, trying to muster the courage, like we were taking our first high dive when the silliness of our behavior struck me. "Oh hell, guys, let's just do this!"

We positioned Fulton as close as possible to the open door, facing forward, and the four of us, one under each arm and leg, hoisted Fulton up and into a seated position on the cabin floor. He jooked himself into a more comfortable position alongside my seat, and then as if to test the fit, he reached up and grabbed the yoke, slowly turning it left, right, forward, and back. Then using his one strong arm, he maneuvered his legs to extend forward so that they could touch the rudders. That done, he nodded. He was ready. I'd never seen anyone so excited, so very ready to go flying.

I climbed in, fitted Fulton with his headset, and ran through the prestart checks. I gave up trying to figure out the intercom setup, so we resorted to hand gestures and the occasional loud verbal exchange. He seemed at ease with his place onboard, and with his door closed, he could see quite nicely out his side window. For now, however, he seemed more interested in what was going on inside.... the instruments and radios and my pre-taxi preparations. From his apparent familiarity and pointed questions, I guessed that he had some experience with flight simulators at home. At the very least, he must have read extensively on the subject.

Questions asked and answered, and clearance received, we made our way to the runway. Fulton sat quietly, listening intently to the radio, keeping close track of all that I was saying and doing. Clearly, he was making the most of his unexpected opportunity. I handed him a folded Florida Sectional map so that he could stay abreast of our course after takeoff. He stared at it briefly, then nodded understanding, quickly refolding it to show the immediate area.

During the run-up, Fulton questioned the specifics of the mag check, prop cycle, and flap extension. Upon explanation, he smiled in understanding as if, for the first time, relating his book knowledge to the hands-on experience of actually *doing* it, seeing it, as it were, for the first time. It was refreshing to experience a passenger with Fulton's inquisitive curiosity and obvious joy of discovery.

At the runway, Fulton followed me through on the yoke as I did the last-minute control check and nodded anxiously when I asked if he was ready. The power came up, and we rolled down the runway. Fulton's attention was riveted out the side window, intent on capturing our first seconds airborne in exact detail. We floated into the air and climbed easily away. Fulton stared quietly while I exited the pattern and headed for the beach. We leveled off and headed south toward the inlet. I felt a tugging on my shirt sleeve... Fulton pointed to himself and then the yoke.

"OK, you got it!", I said, and folded my arms across my chest, passing command of the aircraft to him to do and go as he pleased. I was curious to see how he made the "book to reality" transition when it came to actually *flying* the machine. I was impressed. He maneuvered the aircraft smoothly, his big hand gentle on the yoke as he banked left and right, adeptly putting to practice what he'd read and, I like to think, dreamed.

Even without the map, he seemed well-oriented and turned to fly west toward the river, banking steeply to the right when he needed a better view of the ground, each time making a small correction to his path westward. Approaching the river, he all of a sudden banked hard over to the right, flying a near- perfect turn about a point on the ground, a point clearly significant to him. He looked to me, pointed to himself, and then to the smallish cabin about which he circled. "Your house?... Cool!" I then threw him a thumbs up to acknowledge understanding. He beamed. I noted that no one came outside to wave...

He flew a couple of more circles, then satisfied, turned to the river, and climbed. Going through 3000, he pointed again to me and then to the yoke. "OK, I got it" ... Then he pantomimed with his hands what I can only guess were aerobatic-type figures. I nodded understanding but pointed to the placard on the panel restricting the aircraft from "acrobatic" maneuvers. He nodded sheepishly as if embarrassed at himself for not realizing the restriction. I gave him a standby signal and flew a wing over with my hand to indicate what was coming. Fulton, excited but unsure of just what to expect, braced himself anxiously, holding tightly to my seat on one side and the door handle on the other. I started to give him a "that's not necessary" sort of signal, but as I couldn't think of one, I figured I'd just fly the wingover, and he'd see for himself how benign it could be.

Diving just a bit for speed, I eased it up into a big soft, 2 g wingover, floating near weightless over the top and recovering gently back to level flight. Fulton looked surprised at the unexpected gentleness of the maneuver and quickly indicated I do another... and then another. The third time he followed me through, with two fingers on the yoke, memorizing the view out the side at each second during the maneuver, recording it in his mind for future reference and playback. Satisfied that he understood the details, he again pointed to himself and took the controls. And, dammit, if he didn't fly a near-perfect wing over. I applauded his performance, and we laughed together just for the hell of it. He was an impressive student, and I would have liked to stay up and watch him learn more, but fuel was low and it was time to return to the field.

I pointed to the fuel gauges and mouthed to him, "Take us home".

Fulton was in heaven as he zig-zagged his way back to the airport, periodically checking his position with big left and right banks. Approaching the airport, I took the airplane back and readied it for landing. Fulton sat quietly, watching the flaps extend, and then with two fingers gently on the yoke, he followed me through on the landing, recording every moment from his limited view out the side window.

We taxied back and shut down. Fulton was quiet, somber...almost stoic, as the line guys and I reversed our enplaning procedure and deposited him gently back into his wheelchair. The line guys melted away, a little unsure just what sort of emotion was being displayed and just how to take it.

Fulton maneuvered his chair out in front of the plane and turned to stare at the airplane head-on. He was beaming—such joy in one flight. I've rarely witnessed such an effect. He moved to view the airplane's right side, still with that silly grin plastered on his face. Then all the way around the back, beaming still, as he took it all in. …capturing the moment. I stood out front, waiting patiently for Fulton to complete his post-flight airplane appreciation circuit.

At last finished, he motored his way slowly back out front, stopped next to me, turned one last time to face the airplane…and wept.

Never have I witnessed such a personal response to flight. I put my hand on his shoulder and stood quietly while he sobbed gently, not the least embarrassed, as he released his most private feelings.

Then without a word, he turned, shook my hand, and with tears in his eyes, motored slowly back toward his van. I watched him as he situated himself back into his seat, waved briefly, and drove off.

That was the last I saw of Fulton…well, that's not entirely true. Every so often, when I'm out by the river, I'll fly down low and circle a little home, hoping that maybe a quiet man in an oversized chair will wheel himself outside and look skyward to remember anew the dream he had once lived.

THE REDHAWKS: FROM THE COCKPIT

For the fifth time in as many minutes, I wipe the sweat from my forehead, silently cursing the unexpected delay in the airshow today. Across to my left, wingman Gandt is poised and ready, his canopy opened just a hair to allow some meager ventilation. Then, as if rehearsed, we simultaneously shake our heads in silent mutual frustration at the heat, the delay, the waiting.

ATIS says it's 102 degrees, and it's every bit of that. The runway shimmers in the distance, and the sun's heat burns at the back of my neck through the less than adequately tinted canopy. The black flight suit doesn't help either...

At long last, the radio crackles its clearance. Canopy closed and locked, a quick thumbs up to the lead and three Marchettis roll as one toward the far end of the runway. As Harry lifts off in the lead aircraft, I slide left on the runway, holding my aircraft on the ground a bit longer than usual to establish the proper stepdown. The ground falls away, and the first bits of summer turbulence bite at my wings. With a blind grab for the gear handle and without waiting for a response, I move quickly into position tucked under Harry's right wing.

The air is rough, a consistent and unfortunate fact of summer afternoon airshows. My airplane reacts randomly to the fists of turbulence, sometimes in concert with the lead ship, but most of the time not. My propeller's silver disk slices the air less than 24 inches from leader Shepard's wingtip fuel tank, a little behind and below, and I'm thankful my canopy bow hides the dubious proximity from view. My own tip tank rests comfortably, a yard or so beneath Harry's stabilizer, a scant 4 feet from wingman Bob's, similarly positioned on the left. Thus, my position is defined. Technically referred to as the "Parade" position, we jokingly refer to it as the womb; warm and familiar through 1000 hours of combat with the physics of motion.

We climb and turn out of the pattern. I ease my Marchetti out a few feet and check instruments and gear lights. All is in order as I hear Harry's voice as I slide back into position: "Three thousand feet, ninety degrees to go". And then, "Come to line abreast, landing lights on, Check smoke and fuel". Obediently Bob and I slide out to our wingtip positions as Harry drops the formation toward the runway. A small section of fuselage oilcans on Harry's airplane—the 200-knot indicator.

Seconds later, the three aircraft enter the low altitude turbulence that lies stagnate over the runway—approaching the show center from overhead "Smoke on, standby to pull", plenty of speed, better than 240 knots from the sound of it. The "G" comes on as the nose starts up, and I watch as the horizon tilts awkwardly in my periphery. Approaching the vertical, Harry calls us back to the parade position, and Bob and I hurry to our assigned slots. We arrive in position simultaneously, just past vertical, leads wingtip in front of me once again, locked in its 12-inch bubble of acceptable movement. Over the top now and weightless as Harry rounds the loop in the smooth 3000-foot air, I stare trance-like at the lead airplane, my attention riveted, although to nothing in particular. His airplane fills my view, and my mind reacts automatically, superimposing what is with what should be. Tears of sweat sting at unblinking eyes while hands and feet move in tiny fractions of correction, milliseconds behind an invisible, micro schedule of deviations.

The "G" returns as we bottom out of the cloverleaf. I'm relaxed and cautious under the load; glad for the increased wing loading and, at the same time, tense for the low altitude turbulence I know is there. Harry must be feeling good today. I can see trees rushing by in my periphery and fight hard to ignore the green blurs of distraction. "Rule One", he says glibly, and Bob and I tuck in even closer. You see, we have these two rules of formation flying: "Rule One, never be out of position, and Rule Two, if ever out of position, refer to Rule One".

So, Rule One it is as we arc skyward in our wing over turnaround. The stick goes mushy in the slow air at the top, and my position is altered just slightly to maintain the correct "V" formation as viewed from the crowd. My nose is coming down now... hard. Back in position, the turbulence is at its worst now, unloaded and fast. The right roll is next, and as the nose starts up, I slide in tight, anticipating the marginal power reserve for me on the inside. Harry's wing finally comes down—fast into me as I work the power back under almost zero "G". Approaching the inverted position, my power is at its minimum and I allow my aircraft to creep forward a couple of feet to aid in the downhill acceleration needed on the backside. Bob is out to my left somewhere, but I'm only vaguely aware of him. His bright red Marchetti follows noiselessly along like some Technicolor shadow of its real self. Our wingtips are critical here. Normally four to five feet apart, my shifted position brings them even closer. Downhill once more as Harry slows the roll rate, "playing" the formation back to the ground.

Another big wingover, setting up for the Bomb Burst, a really pretty maneuver that holds special significance for Bob and me. For us, its marks the first chance to relax from the rigors of formation flying.

So, we split and do the "cross", "twinkle" and exit. All more an exercise in timing than anything else, very definitely lacking the intensity of tight formation. It's just as well, though; the toughest is yet to come... the Mirror Roll.

I hurry to join Harry while Bob occupies the crowd with some solo maneuvers.

Aboard in loose echelon, I watch "through" Harry to the airfield below, judging for myself when we should start our turn inbound.

" Ninety degrees to go; call clear".

" I'm clear; smoke on".

Slowly Harrys Marchetti rolls inverted while still in turn. It's a good roll; he hasn't displaced much. Cautiously I slide into position, closer and closer, "mirroring" his airplane a scant five feet canopy to canopy, fins overlapping, precisely one foot to the right of his centerline. I watch Harry through the tinted glass of my upper canopy and chuckle inwardly at the sight of him hanging there, upside down above me, a loose flashlight resting comfortably on the canopy at his head.

Feedback through my control stick is significant and awkwardly proportional to the proximity of the two aircraft. In no other position is it as pronounced, just a foot further away, and the "cushion effect" is drastically reduced, necessitating a higher "body angle" on Harry's airplane and lowering his fin dangerously close to my stabilizer. Movement, any movement from this position, is unacceptable. Paradoxically this is one position where to an extent, the further apart the two aircraft are, the tougher it is to maintain position. My concentration is at its peak now; no room for timidity now. To even complete the maneuver, it must be flown with minimum separation. The lead must be flawless, flying an outside Barrel Roll in as slick a machine as the Marchetti is hard enough. To be smooth about it, predictable about it, and consistent about it is a task for only the best of the best.

After what seems to be an interminable dive, the nose starts up. I am acutely aware of the "G" on the airplane and modify my position just a hair to provide adequate fin clearance. As the nose reaches forty degrees high, I anticipate the roll and establish my position solidly, watching my one foot right of centerline requirement closely. With fins now almost completely overlapping, any movement closer to his center line brings them dangerously close, particularly when he starts his roll. The best rolls are accomplished if I can exactly match his roll rate, especially right at the start. Wings need to remain parallel throughout, with centerline distance adjusted with almost imperceptible rudder input.

At long last, the roll begins. I resist the temptation to overreact to the first signs of roll and work to smoothly match what I have come to know as a "Harry standard rate". Ideally, a touch of a right rudder is initially required, and so it is today. Rolling through the inverted, zero-"G" and floating, the controls loose effectiveness. Almost idle power, but we're committed. The two aircraft were held at bay by the proximity effect—there's no way out now. Harry calls it flying formation on infinity, and I'm not sure what it means, but somehow it seems appropriate.

Our hours of practice pay off nicely and the roll continues steadily while I maintain a cautious anticipation of any deviation. Down the backside and into level flight, I breathe again, my mind shifting gears automatically in preparation for our final maneuvers.

Seconds later, Bob slides into view, and we are again joined as three. Our line abreast sequence goes by uneventfully, and soon we inbound for our final maneuver, the tuck under break. A relatively easy maneuver, visually pleasing more than anything else, and it goes without a hitch.

Rejoined one last time, the gear and flaps extend in unison. I have to force myself to concentrate despite the sense of completion. It's not over till it's over, and any on-again, off-again concentration is a nasty habit to get into.

The three Marchetti's touch down as one, taxi in, and shut down. Canopies open, and for the first time, I realize how exhausting the whole evolution has been. My flight suit is soaked, and my hair is wet. Even the hundred-degree temperature feels good.

The show is over, and the experience is gone. But it seems for all the sweat and effort, something less tangible remains. It's hard to describe, and I'm not even sure it's something that can be put into words. Occasionally, during a show, when things are going right, and the team is well-practiced, my mind will be blank. Whole groups of maneuvers seem to pass without really happening. I find myself thinking, daydreaming actually, about this or that or, most often, nothing at all while line-abreast loops take place in front of me. I'm detached, sort of a casual observer of the whole affair, and what's really interesting is that a lot of the time, these are some of the best-flown maneuvers. There exists a kind of dreamlike automaticness taking place that I don't at all understand... Nevertheless, it does exist, and it makes me sometimes wonder about the "gut" source of knowing; intuitive knowledge, I guess you might say. I imagine that if harnessed, and by that, I mean understood, this knowing without knowing might lead to a higher level or learning where the process and not the information is the really significant thing.

It does come easier, the flying, that is, when mind and body act as one. But I have to think that if the experience itself passes without being realized, can it even be fun anymore? Maybe fun isn't the right word, or maybe it just takes on a new meaning, I don't know. But if I have to give up fun, maybe I'll stick to the sweat-soaked flight and the tension headaches that seem to go along with it all...

HARRY

Harry was a character, a larger than life; never a dull moment, character of the first order. You may love him, or you may hate him, but you couldn't deny that he was one of a kind. Virtually no one was indifferent to him. His legacy abounds with colorful episodes of drama, mirth, and mayhem, some funny, some profound... all memorable, and none in need of embellishment. Those of us fortunate enough to have known Harry were never surprised and always entertained by these unique splashes of his character. But to say he was defined by these stories would do grave injustice to him. He was more than that, more than the sum of his escapades and certainly more than any one author's casual remembrances. He was, amongst many things, an accomplished musician, and in fact, many of his closest friends knew him *only* as that. At Harry's memorial service, for instance, there were dozens of people I had never met before. They were his musician buddies.

One, in particular, made the comment:

"Most of you here knew Harry as an accomplished pilot who also played music... Many of us here knew him as an accomplished musician who also flew planes."

Musician or pilot, he was at his happiest doing either. And to hear the other musicians tell it, he was as adept at playing music as I knew him to be flying airplanes.

He had many interests: a Civil War buff, antique gun collector, and old movie aficionado ...

But from my perspective, as I knew him, he was the consummate aviator...a pilot's pilot...the kind of pilot you could throw him the keys to any airplane and be assured that it would be safe in his most capable hands. From antique biplanes to supersonic jet fighters, it mattered little to Harry. They were airplanes, and he was a pilot. He flew them all like he was born in them, often embarrassing their owners with his immediate ability to extract the most from their airplane, flying each smoothly and skillfully to their envelope's edge and beyond.

I first saw Harry fly at Pennsylvania's Reading Air Show in 1972. I was 18. At the time, Reading was a big deal, and all the biggest air show stars were there... Scholl, Krier, Hoover, a young Gene Soucy, and the Blues with their Phantoms. Harry was there flying with his then partner Larry Kingry in a pair of Waco Meteors, more commonly known today as the SIAI Marchetti, SF 260. Officially they were the Waco Meteor Formation Aerobatic Team, but everyone knew them simply as " Harry and Larry". It was their performance I remembered more than any other. Given the caliber of performers on hand that day, that's saying something.

I remember the wind that day was wicked....30 knots, at least with gusts to over 40. Everyone was struggling, and several performers had canceled for the day. I didn't know what to expect of "Harry and Larry", unfamiliar as I was with both performers and aircraft. To say that I was impressed that day would be an understatement. To this day, I can remember their performance in precise detail. From takeoff to landing, the two were welded together, so close to one another that they seemed like one aircraft. I could hear Harry working the throttle against the turbulence, but never did he move an inch from the perfect two-foot propeller to the tip tank position. Through loops and rolls and their signature maneuvers, the "the mirror roll and loop", they flew as one, locked together in a ballet of aerial artistry such as I'd never seen before or since.

Twelve years later, through serendipity and a chance encounter with a mutual friend, I met Harry. He was in the process of forming another formation team and was interviewing for pilots. We clicked instantly and forged a friendship that lasted for more than 30 years. It was during those 30 years that I bore witness to the myriad stories that were to become part of his colorful legacy. At the risk of oversimplifying Harry's life, I present here some of the events that I consider indicative of Harry's character, wit, and philosophy.

Sometime in 1984, as the Redhawks, we were traveling to a show in Oklahoma when we stopped in Pittsburgh for fuel. As we taxied back out for takeoff, Harry requested takeoff for a flight of three. The tower was clearly hesitant and replied,

"You mean you want to take off in formation?" ... "Uh, yeah, that's right", said Harry...

The tower continued: "I'm not sure we can approve that".

Then Harry, ever tactful, "I don't think it's up to you to deny it".

Tower, rather snidely..."Well, OK, but you'll be taking off at your own risk."

To which Harry replied simply, "When don't we"... and off we went...

And then there was the time when at the after-airshow party, some full of-himself hotshot aerobatic pilot elbowed his way up to Harry at the bar and announced louder than he should have,

"I saw you guys fly today, and lemme just say, anything you can do with that Marchetti, I can do inverted!"

Harry never even looked up from his glass of wine... "OK" he said..."lets land..."

And then there was the time in Wilkes Barre, Pa, when the *armed* Marine guard wouldn't let us in the performer's gate because we hadn't yet received our passes. After several minutes of increasingly heated discussion (on Harry's part), he (Harry) finally blurted out, "OK then, you'll just have to shoot us!!" and promptly drove through the gate damn near, running over the guard's foot in the process (the smarter of us in the car were scrambling to hide on the floor in the back seat).

I remember the time we were trying to top the build-ups on our way home from Oshkosh. 19000 feet and climbing, on the verge of a stall, the three Marchettis could go no higher. Me with no nav and wingman Bob with no gyros, Harry announced, "Hang on," and into the clag we went. He mused later that it was *because* we had no instruments/radio that he was certain we wouldn't lose him. He was right (ask Budd Davisson about that one...he was seated next to me).

Then in South Jersey, somewhere, they had closed the main runway for the air show, and we were forced to land on a *very* rough crossing grass runway. We circled the field while Harry tried unsuccessfully to convince the powers to be that we needed the paved runway. With tempers rising and the bureaucrats on the ground steadfast in their denial, Harry reluctantly acquiesced. Bob and I looked at each other with a tacit understanding of what was to come.

The rough turf runway pummeled our airplanes on landing, threatening to bust something on our landing gear. Harry was livid at being forced to land on such an unsatisfactory runway. He was fuming as we parked our airplanes in front of the "adoring air show crowd", who rushed over with their children, anxious to get a close-up view of the "Supermen in their super airplanes". Well, knowing Harry as we did, Bob and I shut down, got out of the airplanes, and walked quickly in the other direction. Harry, vaulted from the airplane, spewed a continuous string of expletives that had mothers covering their children's ears and old men grabbing their pacemakers. Needless to say, we weren't asked back.

As the Redhawks, we worked all winter one year to perfect a Formation Line Abreast Roll, a maneuver that, at the time, no other team was doing. Not long into the season, we happened to be at a show featuring Team America, a formation team also flying Marchettis. After our performance, Chuck Lischer, Team America Lead Pilot, came up and congratulated us on the maneuver and added, "Our (meaning Team America) airplanes don't have enough power to do that maneuver", to which Harry, with no hesitation replied, "Neither did ours...the first thousand times we tried it."

Watching Harry drive back in the day was something to behold. He spoke a continuous string of criticisms, peppered with expletives, all aimed at every other driver on the road. Once when some offensive driver commented to Harry, "Yeah, well, I've been driving for 40 years and NEVER had an accident!!" Harry calmly replied," Yes, but how many have you caused?"

And finally, those who knew Harry, however, casually, knew what a fanatic he was when it came to his precious Marchetti. Cleaned meticulously and babied with adoring TLC, his Marchetti was spotless, and woe betide any who dared blow dirt on it while taxiing thoughtlessly or pawed at it at air shows, leaving messy fingerprints. So, you can imagine, I'm sure, how I must have felt after running into Harry during a Mirror Roll photo shoot, leaving a small 4-inch crease in Harry's elevator with my rudder. I was devastated and moped around all afternoon, depressed and embarrassed at my sloppy airmanship. Harry never said a word.

That night at the bar, when I was particularly morose, intent on drowning my sorrows, Harry looked at me with his glass of Chardonnay raised as if in toast and said simply, "If you're not f...ing up, you're not trying hard enough" and not another word was ever said about it. Ever...

THE FLYBY

11:50:00 AM - You enter the ground effect at just under 250 mph, two feet from the leader's wingtip, in a 70-degree bank, so far, so good.

Then you notice the bank beginning to increase. You're ready for it, and it only changes a degree or so, but it takes that much to notice. It's a smooth increase—definitely the leads doing and not any turbulence. But whatever the reason, right now, you've got to play catch up. The sooner you can "catch" his bank angle, the better you'll be able to stay with him as he continues to increase his bank. So, you press the aileron into the lead to increase the bank. Because the bank is increasing, and the altitude (hopefully) is remaining constant, the "G" is increasing, which means not only has the stick force changed but the angle of attack has as well. The increased angle of attack produces a change in "P" factor that must be compensated for with the rudder. The increased angle of attack also changes the induced drag that must as well be compensated for, only this time with the power. Of course, the increased power changes several things as well. First, because the pitch of the propeller changes to maintain the selected rpm, both torque and "P" factor change. The "P" factor is corrected for with the rudder as before. Still, it, in turn, produces a rolling moment due to the vertical center of gravity difference and dihedral effect and must be compensated for with the ailerons, which subsequently change the stable position of the ailerons and require further changes in the rudder. This circular sort of rudder/aileron interaction continues in ever-decreasing magnitudes until the next major change occurs or, more probably *when* the next major change takes place. Superimposed over all this is the torque effect caused by the increased blade angle on the now more powerful engine output. So not only is the aileron used to compensate for the rudder input, but simultaneously it is used to counter the effect of increased torque. Not to be forgotten is the gyroscopic precession. Any movement around the lateral axis causes a coupling in yaw which must be allowed for. The movement in pitch, because of the increased "G" sets this off, and the rudder must again be used to compensate. Again, the rudder does its dirty deed of creating a rolling moment due to the vertical center of gravity and must be compensated as before. Further, because of the increased angle of attack on both aircraft, the downwash of the lead's airplane requires an increased angle of attack on the wingman's aircraft. So, in addition to everything else the increased angle of attack due to downwash must be compensated for. Remember also that the downwash increase is taking place linearly but continuously and must be allowed to a differing degree as the bank is increased. This requires a power addition for the increased drag of a higher angle of attack, which, as before, produces changes in torque, p factor and gyroscopic precession as well as slipstream effect. So as before, the rudder, aileron and power must work to correct the major defect, then in turn each must work to dampen the coupling effects each of them has on each other's movements. Additionally, because of the increased bank, the G's have pushed you further into the seat requiring a new visual picture to be compensated for. Even though the airplane hasn't moved, it is up to you to determine, on a continuing basis, just what this new picture needs to look like in order for the two airplanes' positions to not change position relative to each other.

Now, assuming you overshot once high and once low and then again only slightly high and again slightly low trying to capture the roll rate/angle, that's five corrections starting to roll and, similarly, five corrections stopping the roll. That's ten. Now, for each one of them, you have the corrections for adverse yaw produced. Let's say, for argument's sake, that you catch the correction with just one overshoot and then nail it. That brings the total corrections to 20, and so far, we've only dealt with the roll vs. adverse yaw aspect of the flyby. Because each rudder input to correct for adverse yaw also produces its own rolling moment, an overshoot/undershoot correction must be applied to each of the 20 so far corrections bringing the total to 100.

Next, the power corrections: power must be added because of the increased angle of attack/ "G" and turn radius. Assuming a typical five tries to narrow the power to match that required and an associated "overshoot/undershoot/little overshoot/little undershoot/right on" series to nail down the rudder required for "P" factor, that's 25 corrections bringing the grand total so far to 125.

Next is the rolling moment due to vertical CG corrections and the dihedral effect. Because they happen concurrently with the adverse yaw corrections, they produce a 5 series of corrections for each of the 100 already demanded adverse yaw, bringing the total to 625. The 5 power corrections also demand another 5 series correction for torque, which because they couple to affect the rudder and its associated 125 corrections already discussed, now bring the total to 625 x 5 x 5 or 15,625 corrections. Finally, if you include the changing downwash as it affects each wing of your airplane, then you have to address the associated aileron/rudder/roll due to CG/ "P" factor corrections as it affects each of the corrections thus far, that is 15,625x15,625 - or at a minimum 244 million corrections if you could count all that theoretically would be required... And all this assumes smooth air.

Elapsed time so far in the flyby... Three-quarters of a second.

No wonder you sweat.

TERMINAL VELOCITY

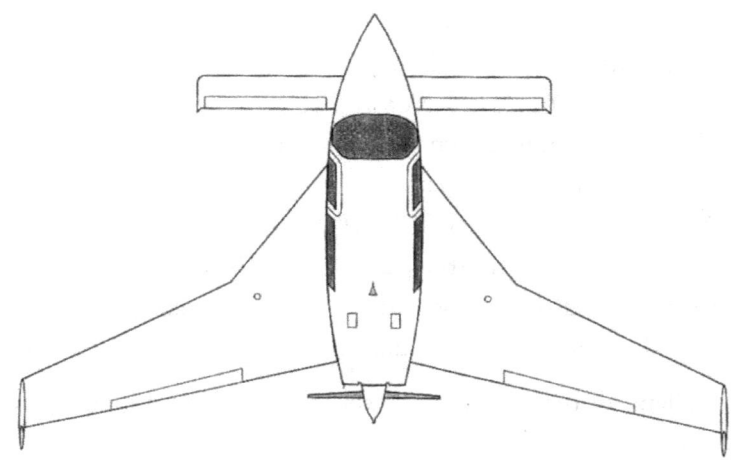

It was a morning like any other in the Florida early springtime... a nondescript dawning to what turned out to be anything but nondescript day. I arrived at the St Augustine Airport early, swung by the FBO, said my hellos to Jim Moser, the proprietor, and drove on to the hanger to ready the airplane for what was to be its final flight in the month-long test program.

I had flown the Velocity twenty times now in half as many days, 25 hours or so, and after nearly 300 stalls of all types, I had acquired the sort of confidence in the canard pusher that I had hoped for. This particular Velocity, a factory build machine, was as clean and slick as they come, and if you can get past the fact that it looks like a giant orange pickle fork flying backward, you might even think it pretty...

...maybe...

But I digress...

I had been engaged by the factory to investigate the high

angle of attack characteristics of the Velocity in an effort to determine its propensity, or more expectedly, its lack thereof, to exhibit "deep stall" or "pitch hang-up" tendencies when subjected to transient episodes of extreme positive angles of attack flight.

A "deep stall", variously referred to as "pitch hang up", "super-stall", or "locked stall", is a relatively rare phenomenon that occurs in some aircraft. When approaching extreme angles of attack (generally well beyond stall), the aircraft, either through "blanketing" or surface stall, exhibits a loss of pitch control effectiveness, rendering the elevator functionally useless, particularly as it relates to stall recovery. If, along with that, the airplane is content to remain in this ultra-high AOA condition, the nose can "hang up" and an "aerodynamically locked" sort of condition can develop wherein the airplane "mushes" along, suffering extreme *angles* of descent (in some cases, dead vertical) while sustaining angles of attack approaching, and in rare cases, exceeding 90 degrees. Descent *rates* vary from deadly to marginally survivable, although, as regards the Velocity's history of deep stall episodes, there is some disagreement as to their exact magnitude. One thing that *is* agreed upon is that unless alternate means of reducing the angle of attack are employed, the descent will generally continue unabated until either luck or the ground intervenes.

Though most of the time associated with the "T Tail" and high-mounted horizontal stab configured aircraft, the deep stall phenomenon has been evidenced in several different canard designs as well. In fact, it happened that on at least two (now three) occasions, a canard-configured aircraft did, it was believed, exhibit the classic 90-degree angle of attack "deep stall fall" all the way to the ground. Much is still unknown about the particulars of these accidents, and reliable feedback was, until recently, unavailable.

Thus, it was to be my task to verify that a properly constructed example, when loaded within prescribed limits and built according to plans, could not display such aberrant behavior. In other words, it was hoped to show that the design was "characteristically incapable" of deep stalling, be it a factory-built example or, as most were, a homebuilt, plans-constructed model.

During the test phase, each of the flight's initial conditions was carefully controlled and documented. The control deflections were verified to be within limits, and the aircraft was fueled to capacity to minimize any CG shift due to fuel sloshing. The aircraft was weighed prior to each flight, and its CG was carefully adjusted, calculated, and logged into my preflight test card.

Early on, a stall matrix was developed to ensure all types of stalls at all allowable CGs were explored and evaluated. We had all our bases covered. Now, we just had to fly the plan.

The idea was to look at stall recovery behaviors in various types of high alpha (angle of attack) scenarios using standard recovery inputs as well as with aggravated, abused and delayed input techniques.

On all previous flights, I couldn't get the airplane to behave anything but conventionally despite my deliberate attempts at ham-fisted, slow-witted airmanship. This particular flight, my twenty-first, was to be the last of the high AOA tests, one in which the CG was adjusted as close as possible to its aft most design limit.

So, after ballasting the aircraft for proper CG and rechecking the weight and balance, I donned my chute, climbed in, and went through the requisite pre-start checks and setups. Taxiing to the runway, I marveled at how smoothly things had gone so far. Not surprising ... after all, it was *expected* to behave normally ...

Right ...

Mistake number one ...

Takeoff and climb-out were uneventful as I turned north along the beach, smoothly climbing to 9500 feet. It was truly a magnificent day ... Florida coast-to-coast visibility, smooth glassy air, and a horizon you could cut yourself on. I was happy with the results thus far, and although I wasn't in love with the airplane, it nevertheless revealed itself to be an efficient and well- behaved design. I *expected* more of the same today ...

Mistake number two ...

I had just completed my thirtieth and final (I thought) stall of the day, a power-on, accelerated, 45-degree bank, cross- controlled stall with a purposely delayed nose-down recovery input. It, as had all the others, dutifully responded to my less- than-optimum recovery inputs and returned itself to wings level, airspeed-increasing flight. Ho hum and yawn ...

That was it ... I was done ... The last box on my last test card filled in, and not a hint of an issue with any of the stalls... I was content ... somewhat bored with the tedium of it all but satisfied nevertheless with the results. It had received my seal of approval, factory expectations upheld. Time to relax ... Time to go home ... Done ... Yes ... For sure now ... Done.

Then ...

Southbound, 9500 ' MSL, 20 miles north of the St Augustine Airport, over the Atlantic Ocean, half a mile offshore

... I thought ... what the hell ... Just one more ... why not ... one more for good measure ... one more ... plain vanilla stall ... low risk ... just one ... for fun ... then ... that will be that ... one more ... for sure ... no really ... one more ... low ... risk ...just ... one ... more ... BIG mistake ...

So ... power back, nose up 10 degrees...hold it ... airspeed falling off... airframe shudder ... there's the pitch down ... aahh... so predictable ... so easy ... ho hum ... release the back pressure ... airspeed increasing ... good ... 90 knots ... Now, aggressive aft stick for the accelerated stall ... nose responds dutifully ... heavy shudder ... five degrees nose high ... nose starts down ... ho hum again ... stick forward to help ... wings level ... stick forward ... Ho hum ... come on ... nose down ... come on down ... forward stick! nose stops ... FULL FORWARD STICK!!! What the ??!?!?! Nose stops at the horizon ... airspeed zero ... AIRSPEED WHAT? WAIT!!!! WHAT!!! AIRSPEED WHAT?? AIRSPEED ZERO!!! CAN'T BE! ... the nose is dead on the horizon ... *dead on the horizon!!* FULL POWER!!! NOSE IS STUCK ... LOCKED!! NO ROLL ... NO YAW ... DEEP STALL! DEEP STALL!! 9000 FEET ... I'm in a pancake fall .... can't be!!! get it down! get it down!! damn!! damn!! damn!! locked ... LOCKED ... SOLID!! Think!! Think!! Keep it together ...! you can do this! *Think*! Try pitch rocking the nose ... stay cool ... rock it ... full aft, full forward ... get it to cycle... full aft stick ... full forward ... full aft ... full forward ... work it in phase ... if I'm moving forward at all this should work... come on you bitch! move!! Nothing!! It's stuck solid! no movement ... move move move ... no luck ... radio ... quick...

"St Augustine ... Velocity ... over the water... deep stall

... tell Jim".

  Back to it ... OK, think ... think ... 8000 feet ... slow decent ... I've got time ... gotta get the CG forward... unbuckle

... slide forward under the panel ... one hand on the side stick ... full nose down ... NOTHING ... 7500 FEET ... think dammit ... I reach back and toss a sandbag of ballast under the panel on the right side ... STILL NOTHING! What else? What else? remember ... come on ... come on ... got it!!! roll out of it ...that's it!! of course! roll it out! full lateral stick right - nothing ... full left ...

nothing … right … nothi … WAIT ! something there … Tiny bit of roll … gotta get the timing right … got to have it just right … Must have at least a tiny bit of forward velocity … left stick, right stick … left stick … 7000 feet … airspeed zero … roll building up … got to get the roll timing just right to … left right, left right… bank angle, bigger each time … incrementally bigger, but bigger… LEFT RIGHT … LEFT RIGHT LEFT RIGHT, MORE BANK, MORE BANK, 30 DEGREES, 40 DEGREES. WHEN IT GETS TO 45, I'M GOIN' FOR IT … LEFT RIGHT, LEFT RIGHT… THERE IT IS 45 DEGREES!!! GO!!! FULL FORWARD, FULL LEFT … full rudder … TIGHT LEFT SPIRAL … WHY ISN'T THE NOSE COMING DOWN… THIS CAN'T BE!!! 6500 feet … tighter,

tighter … spiraling down fast … 6000 feet … airspeed 40!!! 40???!!! What the F !!!! COMING DOWN FAST ALTIMETER UNWINDING … PRECIOUS ALTITUDE … NO GOOD … TRY AND ROLL BACK OUT OF IT … ROLL OUT OF IT

… IT STAYS LIKE THIS AND I'm for sure gonna have to jump

… FULL RIGHT, FULL AFT … SLOWLY … SLOWLY … BACK TO LEVEL!!! BACK TO THE WINGS LEVEL DEEP STALL FALL … THIS CAN'T BE HAPPENING! AIRSPEED ZERO … AGAIN!!! SLOW DECENT … THIS IS A DREAM

… JUST CAN'T BE!! OK … TIME TO GET SERIOUS … GOTTA JUMP … JUMP … WAIT … STILL HAVE TIME … ONE LAST TRY … 4500 …

It's a last resort … but, it *could* work … just maybe … CG is the key … I *know* it is! Open the pilot side hatch … FLAT AS A PANCAKE … No wind … absolutely no sense of motion … no sense of falling … The engine roars somewhere in the back of my mind … prop cavitates its displeasure with the whole thing …

MY GOD! THIS IS BIZARRE!! NO WIND ... ABSOLUTELY NO SENSE OF MOTION! Stand up ... go on ... do it ... unstrap ... do it! stand up on the seat ... DAMN ... forgot to unplug the headset ... OK, now stand up ... no relative wind! bizarre! one foot on the wing, one on the seat ... 4000 feet ... leaning forward ... still no apparent wind

... It's as if I'm suspended in midair ... encased in a static air bubble, floating lazily like some "Velocity" shaped hot air balloon.

Leaning forward, inching my hands toward the canard and across 4000 feet of open-air drop...CG has *got* to be forward now!! More forward, slowly, more forward, on to the wing ... leaning across the expanse of air between the wing and canard ... reaching forward, left hand now on the canard

inching forward ... right hand wrapped across the forward nose cone ... both hands tight ... body stretched out to full length ... eyes locked on to the horizon, looking for some ...ANY signs of nose down movement ... ANY movement at all!!! COME ON!! CG has *got* to be way forward ... looking for the first sign of movement ... right foot hooked on to the windshield bow, ready to yank me back inside ... BUT, the airplane IS LOCKED SOLID ... stubbornly adhering to its newfound comfort zone ...

I could almost hear it laughing at me ... DAMN AND DAMN!!

I give up and pull myself back inside ... 3500 feet ... Try the roll phasing again, this time to the right ... maybe with the lower altitude ... I've got to get the bank steeper ... Time's running out ... Left right, left right, left right ... bank increasing each time, 45 degrees, and it'll go no steeper ... here we go! This time, Full right, FULL NOSE DOWN, FULL right RUDDER ... This has *got* to work!!! spiral wrapping up ... Tighter, tighter, airspeed still hovering around an impossible 40! Altitude unwinding ... 3000 ... May have to get out ... Over water ... Yea, right ... Reverse the controls   reverse the controls ... get it back to the flat fall ... Magically, it returns to the flat fall ... once again chuckling at my feeble attempts to corral its insidiousness.

Radio ... "Jim, I may have to get out"...

Out of ideas ... THINK! THINK! Nothing left ... 2500 ... Stay or go ... stay or go? Strangely relaxed ... thinking ... hmmm, what else is there to do? ... jump First jump over water ... Saw two guys lost like that in the Navy ... look at it again ... nose is up five degrees ... Wings are level ... Yaw rate, zero ... Impossibly slow decent ... Can' t be!! Staring out at the beach ... Pancake ... 2000 ... Stay or go ... stay or go ... Stay stay stay ... 1500 feet ...

Radio: "I'm gonna ride it in to the water" ...

1200 ... strap in ... leave the hatch open ... don't want it to jam ... 1000 ... flat fall ... hold everything ... can't afford a recovery at this point ... too low ... 500 ... facing the beach ... don't move ... stay ... stay just like you are ... don't move ... stay steady ... don't recover now ... stay steady ... hold it ... hold it ... at 50 feet, I get the first real visual of just how fast I'm coming down ... and ... THIS IS IT!! SAAAAH ... MACK!!!!!

The water comes up fast, and I slam into the ocean way

harder than I expected ... flat as a pancake ... *straight down!!!* seat collapses on the right side ... ribs crunch! UGH !!! prop splinters ... engine stops ... radio dies ... and just like that it's over ... I'm down ... down and alive ... alive ... and dry ... breathe ... breathe ... yes ... alive. and floating ... safe ... yes ... alive ... unhurt ... alive ...

I sit ... I breath ... I stare ... waves slosh ... beach goers gawk ... airplane bobs ... splish ... splash ... splish ... splash...

HO...   LEEE...   CRAP!!!!

I sit for just a moment trying quite unsuccessfully to digest the ridiculousness of what just happened. It's all a jumble of nonsense in my head ... at odds with what I *thought* I knew about reality ... what I thought I knew about aerodynamics ... I'm completely flummoxed ... maybe I'm dead? Hmm ... how would I know?

I'm sitting there waxing philosophically when it hits me ... I never radioed my position ... Damn! Jim is probably out looking ... but where??? the river? the Ocean ... north or south? I could be anywhere. I try the radio again, but the battery dislodged on impact, tearing itself out of its mounts and rendering itself out of reach behind the seat back bulkhead.

Hmmm ... half a mile or so from the shore ... could probably swim it ... ribs feel ok enough ... I think ...

First things first ... battery switch off ... unstrap ... headset off ... get out ... floating nicely ... No visible damage except for the shattered wood prop ... cockpit dry ... climb up on the fuselage and sit ... waiting ... waiting ... what now ... some kid on the beach waving ... I wave back .... looks further than I thought ... and so I continue to wait ...

Five minutes .... ten minutes ... tick tock ... tick tock ... then ... Noise overhead ... louder and louder ... a twin ... Ah ... Beach Baron overhead ... circling ... lower, lower ... turns out it's an old Navy buddy, Andy ... he'd been listening to the whole thing and somehow has lucked onto my position ... helped, no doubt that the airplane was the only bright orange thing bobbing around in the ocean that day ... minutes later a 182 shows up ... It's Jim, and I'm suddenly worried about the two of them flying into each other ... such irony ... Jim flies by low ... wave top height ... I signal a thumbs up, and he retreats to safer altitudes just as a Navy H60 appears on the horizon. Andy is coordinating the "rescue" from on high, no doubt...

The chopper's whop whop whop grows steadily louder, and in short order, the H60 is on scene stirring a swirling mist of ocean saltwater obscuration as he slowly edges closer ... rescue swimmer, feet out the door, ready to jump ... I throw him a quick thumbs up and signal OK ... no sense both of us getting wet ... A thumbs up in return and down comes the rescue horse collar... plops it in the water about 25 feet away ... and I guess I'm gonna get wet after all ... stow the chute and headset ... One last look around the cockpit ... all is quiet ... dive in and make my way to the collar ... Navy training kicks in ... thumbs up to the winch guy and up I go ... Laugh inwardly at the sight of my "airplane boat" bobbing softly with the waves, now more boat than plane .... hope someone comes soon to rescue *it* ... up and up I go ... Strong hands pull me in ... safely ensconced aboard ... Navy corpsman quickly checks me ... says I'm good to go ... "where to?", they ask ... and so ... next stop, St Augustine Airport ... What service! I owe these guys ...

I step off the chopper on the AeroSport ramp at St Augustine like it happens every day. None of this has sunk in yet. I walk into the FBO, silly with life, dripping wet but relatively unscathed, with an aviation story of a lifetime ... a story even, to this day, I have a hard time believing ... and thirsty, all of a sudden, for some of that Happy Hour "Crown" I know Jim has stashed in his desk. I pour myself a shot ... and then another. Exhaustion overtakes me. I sit and think and then, tired of thinking, I just sit. What a day. What a day, indeed ... I put my head on the desk and close my eyes in complete disbelief and exhaustion.

Epilogue

The airplane, other than a busted prop, a salt waterlogged engine, and some minor fiberglass damage to the wheel pants, the aircraft was essentially unhurt, and in fact was ready to fly again three weeks later.

To Velocity's great credit, the spin experts up at Langley were brought in, and the deep stall issue was thoroughly investigated and tested. Much was learned, if not completely understood, about the deep stall phenomenon and its bizarre behavior. Requisite modifications and retrofits were made to the plans, and pertinent data were supplied to builders. To date, no other incidences of deep stall have been reported.

The FEDs, after hearing my account, really didn't know what to do with this one ... and as far as I know, the report is still stashed away in some "X-File" type data base somewhere ...

C. S. PASCARELL

THE PARISIAN ADVENTURE

Or How I Survived a Calamitous Crossing… Twice.

There are adventures, and then there are adventures. And then there are damn fool escapades. The funny thing is, what passes for adventure when you're 28, can seem like a damn fool escapade when you're 58. So, I guess it depends on your perspective what you'd call an over-ocean flight to the Paris Air Show in a prototype corporate jet aircraft with less than 25 hours on it... no nav, no anti-ice and no pressurization. For me back then... no question... it was all adventure. Sure, it was my job, but that was secondary to the promise of world-class excitement it portended. Challenge, experience, risk, and reward. It had it all. I didn't, for a second, regard what were clearly red flags.

Lest you think my attitude entirely flippant, I can assure you my approach was not completely cavalier. My experience crossing the North Atlantic to this point was limited to coach class service on a Pan Am 74'. Given the magnitude of this undertaking and being saddled with the weighty responsibility of caretaking the company's sole product, with the economic fate of the entire Company potentially at risk, it was an obligation I did not take lightly. The Company's very future itself could well depend on a successful Paris Air Show experience, and I was determined not to be a liability to that end. I needed help and wasn't ashamed to ask for it. I thus engaged the services of my friend and aviation writer, Bill Cox, a veteran Ocean flyer with dozens of crossings in all types of general aviation singles and twins, to be my copilot and logistics insurance during the crossing. He proved to be a valuable resource as well as steady, unflustered help when things started to fall apart.... As they did...on several occasions...

I had been involved in the development of Ed Swearingen's SJ30 since its inception. It was an exceptional design, revolutionary in its efficiency, and the first of the small corporate jets to be designed specifically to take advantage of the then-new Williams FJ44 jet engines. Featuring cruise altitudes in the mid-forties and a fuel burn more typical of turboprops, it seemed the ideal engine - airframe marriage. Imagine a Mach .82 jet flying in the 40s, burning less than 300 pounds a side—truly unprecedented performance. I joked with Ed that the toughest thing we would have to deal with would be to convince corporate jet jockeys that 1000 pounds was a lot of gas.

The prototype SJ30 I was to fly to Paris was built as an experimental development vehicle. As such, many systems you'd consider necessary, or at least nice to have, in this type aircraft, and for this type of mission, were missing. For instance, there was no autopilot, wing deice, windshield deice, and no navigation other than Loran and ADF/DME. Further, outfitted with various flight control, performance, and systems recording equipment, it was considerably heavier than what the future production articles were designed to be—a good 1000 pounds over design gross after we got all our luggage, equipment, and spare parts stowed and full fuel loaded.

But all that said, I liked the airplane, I liked flying it and enjoyed the challenge that experimental flight test offered. Taking it to Paris was a different sort of challenge, one step removed from flight test, but as it turned out, one fraught with challenges all its own.

San Antonio to Bangor

Topped off with 5000 pounds of fuel, the SJ30 had range enough to make the crossing with minimal stops, and we flight planned it thusly. Little did we realize our well-considered plan wouldn't survive the first leg. Our planned first stop was in Bangor, Maine. There we would overnight, after uploading the required over-ocean survival equipment - Rafts, emergency radios and subsistence foodstuffs all designed to help us survive any catastrophe that we were likely to have befall us.

And so, in the predawn hours of that first day, Bill and I stowed what gear we needed to take, topped off the fuel, and settled aboard for what was planned to be a 4-hour, 30-minute flight to Bangor. Taxiing out, I wondered absently about the takeoff performance given our over-gross condition but felt confident in the airplane's ability to deal successfully with it... at least with both engines running. Its single-engine performance was, to this point, not looked at too specifically, and I had only a gut sense that the airplane would perform sufficiently well under the given circumstances. I hoped we wouldn't get to test that hypothesis.

The takeoff, as it happened, was uneventful, and the ensuing climb to flight level 330, though increasingly stately, was uneventful as well. It was a perfect day for the trip...clear skies, unlimited visibility, and a 50-knot tailwind to boot. We should arrive in Bangor early and with fuel to spare.   Sweet.

We had just entered that phase of long cross-country flying when boredom started to set in. I was roused from my inappropriate revery by the intermittent cycling of what I knew from experience was the landing gear hydraulic motor. Bill noticed it as well and looked quizzically at me for an explanation. I had only to say "landing gear hydraulics", knowing he was experienced enough to understand what the problem was and how it could potentially affect us. In this airplane, and unlike most others, the landing gear had no uplocks and was designed to be held up with trapped hydraulic fluid. When occasionally the pressure would bleed down, the gear motor would cycle on for just half a second or so to suck it back up into the wells. So, it wasn't uncommon to hear the motor cycle from time to reseat the gear, but it was equally clear that it most definitely should not be cycling as often as it, in fact, was. At first, it was every ten minutes, then every 5 minutes. When it started cycling every 20 seconds or so, I knew we had a problem, and just like that, I wasn't so bored anymore...

The more optimistic side of me hoped it was the pressure switch that was acting up. The more pragmatic me knew it was something more...a leak, more than likely, maybe an errant bypass...but almost certainly, trouble. While it could have been the switch, I couldn't take that chance and had to, for safety's sake, assume the worst. And the worst was decidedly not good. A leak meant we were losing hydraulic fluid... fluid used to operate the flaps and leading-edge devices, and, more significantly, to lower the landing gear. The flap part of the problem didn't immediately concern me. I had made no flap landings before with the airplane, with no issues. And being right atop Memphis with its two-mile runways, a no-flapper would be the least of my concerns. It was the potential problem with the landing gear that had me worried. I made the decision pretty quickly to lower the gear while we still had pressure and fluid, get it on the ground, and *then* worry about troubleshooting the problem. I was disappointed with the disruption to our flight plan, but better safe than sorry, and as we had plenty of time to get to Paris, it was an easy call to set down and get it fixed.

So, we called Memphis Center, told them we'd be landing in

Memphis, slowed in the descent, and threw the gear out....

Nothing....

A minute later... Still nothing...

Shit...

I looked at Bill... His expression mirrored my own... A "you got to be kidding me " sort of look that we both knew meant things were about to get interesting. I knew the gear partially extended ... I could hear from the wind noise that much. But with no green gear down lights, I had to assume the gear was stuck somewhere in transit. The good news was we had plenty of gas, plenty of daylight, good weather and were right smack on top of Memphis. So, we had time... Or so I thought...

We ran through the standard tricks to try and extend the stubborn landing gear: slowing the airplane to let the gear free fall into position, yawing the airplane to engage air loads to our benefit, and "G ing" the airplane in an effort to pull the gear out and to full extension. Nothing... We even tried a couple of Tower flybys to get at least an *idea* of what we were dealing with. The Tower did its best, but as this *was* a prototype, the tower really had no idea what to look for, and the best we got from them was, well...the gear was definitely *not up*.

There was always the emergency nitrogen blow-down bottle, but as that isolated the hydraulics from the other airplane systems, I wanted to exhaust other avenues first.

Other avenues exhausted; it was time to seek the advice of the professionals. After all, who better to get involved than the designer himself? I mean, what good is it to work for the man if I can't call him on the phone when things start to fall apart?

I handed the airplane to Bill and grabbed my Jeps to look up the local AIRINC* frequency. While Bill flew a big lazy circle around the Memphis airport, I quickly called New York AIRINC and, in pretty efficient order, established a phone patch direct to Ed Swearingen's office back in San Antonio. Ed answered right away and was quickly brought up to speed on the situation. He thought a moment and, in a rapid-fire, asked, how 'bout this, did you do this, did you do that, did you try this?

"Yep, yep, yep and, yep…twice."

Then in resignation, he said, "Well, go ahead and blow the gear down."

With Bill still flying, I said, "OK, here goes", and with that, I pulled the emergency gear handle. My eyes locked on to the gear lights insisting my will on them to go green.

Nothing…

Shit and damn…

"Ed?… no good". Silence on the line… Then…

Ed - " How slow have you gotten?" Me- " About 110… flaps 30…"

(We'd been flying around pretty slow, at flaps 30, in an effort to reduce the air loads and allow the spring assist on the gear to more easily push the gear to full extension and lockdown.).

Ed - "Go to forty… slow it right on down". Me -"Roj".

I took the airplane from Bill, slid the flap handle into the forty notch, and slowed to the onset of the buffet.

Me - "Nothing Ed…"

Ed - " Standby".

I passed the airplane back to Bill, reached behind my seat, and grabbed a handful of loose-leaf papers and system diagrams that served as our operating and maintenance manual. I was particularly interested in the emergency hydraulic override switches and their relation to the system plumbing. I had the diagrams spread out on my lap, tracing the fluid path, trying to make sense of it, when in my periphery, I noticed the control yoke steadily rotating to the right as if beginning a right turn. That's odd...I thought we were in a left orbit   and then I looked over at Bill ...WHAT THE   the yoke was now fully deflected to the right!!! I looked up and saw us rolling through 60 degrees of BANK. TO THE *LEFT*.!!! SHIT! I grabbed the yoke while instinctively crossing up the throttles.... FULL POWER ON THE LEFT, IDLE ON THE RIGHT, while simultaneously mashing full right rudder. The airplane skewed and slid in this ridiculous, fully deflected effort to arrest the uncommanded roll. Christ almighty! What the shit is going on! Then it struck me ...DAMN! and DAMN again!!! How could I *not* have thought of that?! A quick check out at the wings confirmed my fears... What was an inconvenience a minute before just became gravely critical. With the hydraulics bypassed and effectively isolated, the *slats* were no longer held locked up and were free to extend under the aerodynamic loads. Our high angle of attack effort to reduce air loads had sucked the inboard slat on the right wing to the full extended position. With no left-right interconnect and no asymmetry protection, we were stuck with an asymmetric roll condition barely controllable with full lateral control deflection. Things were instantly critical. We were on the ragged edge of disaster. We both knew that if that right *outboard* slat came out, we'd lose the airplane...there just wasn't enough roll authority to handle it.... And us, with no chutes...

Ed - "Have you thought about ...."Me - "NOT NOW!!! WE GOT TROUBLE !!"

So, there we were, full power on one engine, idle on the other, the controls fully deflected to the right.........left engine over-temping and unable to maintain altitude...

Me - "Ed, we're puttin' this thing on the ground...NOW!!! We got inboard slat asymmetry; we're maxed out on lateral control deflection and can't handle any additional rolling moment. The wrong slat comes out and we're finished."

Ed - " Oh....I see ", just as calm as he could be...

We were flying about 110 knots and barely keeping it together. At least I know 110 works.... for now...Any slower and we may suck that other slat out. Any faster and....well, who knows? I don't know anything else for sure, so 110 is gonna be it to touchdown. Gear or no gear, we're coming in...

I switched to Memphis Tower, declared the emergency, and spiraled down, planning our descent to intercept a close in the final. Bills was calling out speeds and altitudes while I maneuvered to set up a quarter-mile final.

Left engine - red line hot and increasing.... great...

Ed - "You'll have nose gear steering, regardless of the main gear position."

Then, ever the pragmatist...

"If you touchdown at 105 or so, you'll grind down the outboard flap and wing tip, but if the nose gear is extended at all, you should be able to keep it on the runway."

Such faith....

We were descending through 1500 feet, trying desperately not to disturb the tender balance of forces keeping us right side up when I had one last thought:

" Bill, d*on't do it now*, but when I give you the word, hit both the hydraulic overrides. I'm going to wait till we're just about to touch down and try one last ditch attempt to scavenge whatever fluid we can for the gear. it may extend the critical slat, but we'll be close enough to the runway that I can just stuff it on the ground before the asymmetry rolls us over."

Bill has got his fingers poised above the two switches, calm and collected like he thinks I got it all under control.

We roll out on the final. I could see the crash trucks, midfield, waiting...I hoped to disappoint them. I stayed locked on to 110 knots and crossed the threshold at 30 feet or so... In the flare... 10 feet... .5 feet. "Not yet Bill... Not yet"... 2 feet...

"waaaait...." 1 foot... "NOW!! HIT EM !!" He mashed the switches just prior to touchdown... clunk, clunk...wham. gear's down!! three greens, slats slam out, and

touchdown ...just that fast... ENGINES TO CUTOFF... Just in case.... rolling out, I cringe, waiting for the gear to collapse... three green and steady... Three greens and steady... Cautiously...

"Bill, I think we did it....

"Holy crap! " He agrees, "I believe we did".

We rolled to a stop on the high-speed turnoff surrounded by crash crew, ready at any moment for our luck to run out and our main gear to fold up. I jumped out of my seat, opened the cabin door in the back, and leaped out to secure the gear, just in case, a couple of "c" clamps from the crash guys toolbox to hold the over-center links in place did the trick, and in pretty short order we were ready to be towed clear of all runways and onto the maintenance hangar where we'd be safe to fly another day.

Disaster averted, I relaxed in the cockpit during the tow, reflecting on the near calamity, wondering what exactly went wrong, how it would be fixed, and what other adventures were in the offing. I closed my eyes...only 5000 miles to go...one way...sigh...

Airplane safely ensconced in the hanger. A quick call to Ed with the good news, room full of engineers cheering in the background, and Bill and I headed for the Airport Marriott bar. All in all, an exciting if not productive first day.

Ed called to say he would be arriving first thing in the morning in one of Bill Lear Jr's jets. I tried to forget about airplanes for the rest of the evening. The Vodka helped...

Bill and I arrived at the hangar early the next morning, just as Ed was pulling up in the Lear. The SJ was already up on jacks, and a crew of mechanics was busy pulling panels, flashlights at hand, investigating the previous day's problem. Ed, in typical "Ed" fashion, arrived at the scene with a potential answer to the problem. It seemed as though our problem was actually two problems. The emergency blow-down system had been just slightly misrigged, and during the climb out had slowly slipped to allow bypass of the normal hydraulic system, but not quite enough to actuate the blow-down bottle. With the hydraulics effectively bypassed, there was no way to repressurize the system when the gear started to sag. Hence the almost constant cycling of the motor. The other issue was simpler but more problematic. The nitrogen precharge for the blowdown system was just too weak to extend the gear with any kind of air load on it. These kinds of development issues were expected and unavoidable, although it would have been nice to have it happen closer to home and without the pressure of having to get somewhere...particularly halfway around the world. The good news was that both problems were easily remedied, and by that afternoon, we were back in business.

We ran off to pack while the crew readied the airplane for departure. Flight plan filed and gear restored, we climbed back aboard, anxious to get to Bangor before nightfall, not the least bit intimidated by the near disaster that threatened us the day before. Aaah, youth...

We had just enough daylight left to make Bangor, so without any fanfare, we said our goodbyes, "see you in Paris", and launched on our second leg of our over-ocean adventure. Climbing out, I was relieved to see the landing gear and flaps retract normally, hydraulics nominal and just the very occasional cycling of the gear motor...just as it should...all was in order. At 15000 feet, I ran through my standard check of engine gauges and system parameters—more trouble. A check of cabin altitude showed it was 12000 feet and climbing—crap. Level off, recycle the bleeds, tell ATC, and recalculate fuel burn and range. Sigh. We could still make Bangor, but tomorrow's Bangor to Reykjavik leg was out of the question. Fortunately, Bill was familiar with the "lesser" airports along the way, and although I wasn't thrilled with the prospect of stopping 3 or 4 more times than was planned, I was glad we had that contingency covered.

We stayed at 12 thousand and canceled with Center, content to Loran and DR our way to Bangor VFR, happily enjoying the CAVU weather luck afforded us along the way. En route, Bill and I discussed our "other airport" options for the next day's Bangor to Reykjavik leg, Gander or Goose Bay initially, then, depending on the weather, either Narsarsuaq or Sondrestrom Fiord,

Greenland. From there, Reykjavik was a pretty simple jump. Navigation, however, was going to be a problem. The Loran is effectively useless in the more northern latitudes, and our ADF (back then, the primary means of navigating when way up north) was worthless outside 25 DME due to an antenna mounting issue. Remember, this was before the days of GPS. We did, however, have DME.... Oh yay...

It was more exciting this way, unfamiliar as I was with any of those places, but my first and only priority was to get the plane to Paris in one piece. A really long leg, showing off the airplane's magnificent capabilities, would have been a nice plus, but such was not to be, and neither Bill nor I wanted to take time in Bangor to troubleshoot the pressurization and ADF problems, and possibly risk losing the perfect weather forecasted for the next couple of days.

The Bangor stop was an exercise in paperwork and red tape administration. Emergency and overwater equipment had to be rented, documented, inspected, and stowed securely aboard. Bill had connections and was assigned the lead on that front. I started a back-of-the-envelope weight and balance calculation based on our new cargo and, after twice figuring it out, decided I really didn't want to know after all. I called San Antonio and spoke briefly with Ed about the pressurization issues, our timetable, and our decision to press on while we had the weather on our side. He agreed fully, only slightly disappointed at our inability to take full advantage of the SJ's long-range capabilities. We also talked candidly about the increased possibility of breaking down (because of the additional stops) in some godforsaken corner of Greenland's frozen wasteland, unable to effect repairs, relegated to sitting out the Paris Show, waiting for parts to arrive by dog sled. Further, and more importantly, I hoped that I wouldn't have to make the decision whether or not to continue to Paris with a less than satisfactory airplane should additional problems arise.

We left Bangor the next morning under sunny skies, with unlimited visibility and renewed faith in the success of our missions despite being nearly 1500 pounds over gross. The airplane nevertheless performed beautifully, and in short order, we were leveled at 12000 feet, readying ourselves for the challenges that lay ahead. We knew our Loran would slowly lose its accuracy as we flew north, and equipped as we were with no other means of "new age" navigation, we reset our compass, opened our topographical maps, and stood by to practice the navigation of 50 years; hence, Ded reckoning. Ded for "deduced", as in heading, wind, and airspeed used to deduce our track across the globe. Checkpoints along the way would provide a check as to our mathematical guesswork as well as input with which to modify our assumptions and update our position... That was all great until we coasted out Overwater. We were completely dependent on our calculations, and that, along with any accuracy we were able to exact from our overland portion was all we had to work with. I reflected that perhaps, "reduced" reckoning might be a more appropriate term for that phase of our journey.

As it happened, the flight north along the ragged Canadian coastline was smooth and, thankfully, disaster-free. We should have been paying closer attention to our time-speed-distance calculations, but the superior visibility made "map in hand - eyes out the window" navigation too easy and too much fun to pass up.

Gander's ash-grey 10000-foot runway came into easy view almost 50 miles out, right on schedule. Cleared for the "visual" 20 miles out, I converted our en-route descent into a close-in final, rolling wings level in the flare. Touching down, I let our overweight landing roll to full length to save tires and brakes, something now even more critical given the added stops in, shall we say, less-than-hospitable places.

After landing, I readied the airplane for fueling while Bill talked with the metro (weather) guys about the forecast conditions en route to our next stop, Narsarsuaq, Greenland. Narsarsuaq is an interesting stopover and one I, paradoxically, was both looking forward to and, at the same time, hoping to avoid. Precariously positioned at the southernmost tip of Greenland, its single north-south runway runs uphill north, smack into the face of a twelve-thousand-foot glacier sitting omnipotent and immovable just off the runway's end, so significant is the slope of the runway that virtually everyone considers it a one-way-in, the other-way-out sort of affair... As overloaded as we were, we certainly did.

Further, the weather there is as unpredictable as any place on Earth. A forecast was at best a wild guess, and stories abound of clear forecasts turning to crap in a matter of minutes, leaving arrivals the option of shooting a less than inviting approach, diverting back to mainland Canada or more north in Greenland to Sondrestrom Fiord - a joint use Military/Civilian field. At the time, the only approach into the field was an NDB/DME straight-in approach with minimums not at all commensurate with how the weather usually turns out. When VFR, the approach is a magnificent sight to behold. From the south, the course guides you down, finally threading its way between majestic fiords rising vertically on either side of the centerline, seemingly close enough to touch. But, as beautiful as it is in visual conditions, I imagine it is quite unnerving to fly when IFR. The approach utilizes NDB/DME guidance, and anyone familiar with the ADF's notoriously erratic behavior, knows that accuracy is not one of its strong suits. The approach publishers must have realized this as well, as evidenced by their Bold-faced admonishment on the face of the approach plate. Words to the effect "If you are not intimately familiar with this approach procedure, do not attempt" are printed in conspicuous view right on the face of the approach plate. I wasn't happy about it, but given the current state of our airplanes "lack of readiness" and our increasingly critical timetable, we pressed on with all the caution we could muster and all the extra gas we could carry.

So, armed with the metro's caveats, we blasted off, headed north to our frozen wasteland next stop, silently praying the weather, airplane, and pilot fortitude would hold together long enough to get us into and, more importantly, out from Greenland's icy cold grip and onto the decidedly more hospitable Reykjavic, Iceland.

The weather, as it happened, was absolutely magnificent en route to Narsarsuaq, and though we were forewarned that things could turn nasty in a hurry, we nevertheless pressed on, blithely unconcerned with the potential hazards that lay in wait, anxious and confident to press on to Paris...

The approach, threading our way up the fjords, was a sight to behold, as stunningly beautiful VFR as I imagine it would be, downright intimidating, IFR. At the same time, the NDB tracking was typically NDB-ish, and were it not for the clear skies and unlimited visibility, the ominous proximity of the fjord's shear cliff boundaries would have only served to increase our already heightened trepidation.

We moved with alacrity, anxious to get airborne before the notorious weather shift reared its ugly head. We were airborne in pretty short order, happy to have been saved from the "infamous weather swap of Narsarsuaq" and safely on our way to our overnight stay in Reykjavik, Iceland.

Reykjavik was a hub of activity, hosting a slew of brand- new and prototype aircraft, all headed to Paris. For us, things were beginning to settle down. A welcome rest was afforded us that night at the airport Loftleidir Hotel despite the 24 hours of daylight the northern latitudes and time of year had in store for us.

The next morning fuel and weather checks were uneventful, and we were soon airborne and headed to Paris. We made a brief stop in Prestwick Scotland to refuel, and it was on to Paris. Once again, CAVU conditions prevailed, and it began to look as if the worst was behind us.

At last. Le Bourget Airport, Paris, France - The largest Airshow/exhibition on the planet, 50-something countries, 20 different languages, and the latest military hardware - all on active display. This was my second Paris Airshow, having flown there two years previous in a small turbine-powered trainer, the SA32T. I was impressed then and remained so this time.

The very first thing I did was seek out the Trimble Navigation people in the exhibition hall. After explaining our "no nav, dead reckoning" flight across the pond, they graciously loaned us one of their, then new, portable GPS' and a spare battery. We were lucky we had the severe clear conditions on the way over, but I sure didn't want to count on that sort of luck continuing.

The airshow brief each day was short and sweet, forty-five minutes, 2 languages, and 20-plus countries. Everyone knew what was expected of them as well as the consequences of anything less than complete professionalism.

To wit: When issued a takeoff time for your demo, it was expected that you'd be at the runway, ready to go. And when cleared for takeoff, it was expected that 5 minutes later, you'd have landed and taxied clear of the runway. Not 5 minutes and 5 seconds - but 5 minutes. They are, to put it succinctly, no BS. Screw up at all, and you will hear about it the next day at the briefing. Screw up a second time, and you will be done for the week; no appeals, no whining, you're finished. So bust the minimum altitude, fly outside the "box", land after your 5 minutes is up, and it doesn't matter if your Joe Blow in a little acro plane or General Dynamics' F-16. You're finished for the week.

It reminded me of flying into Chicago's O'hare airport. Those controllers are the very best, and they don't put up with anything less than complete professionalism. It's funny, but when constraints like that are imposed on you, and the consequences are real, you necessarily perform at a higher level. It is because of these imposed limits that Paris is able to put in the air 40-50 demos per day.

So, except for an on-takeoff engine failure in the SA 32T, the show went pretty well. I should explain. The turbine engine in the SA 32T unwound at 200 feet on takeoff, just as the gear was retracted. So…. Put the gear down, turned a dogleg right, and landed on the cross runway. No big. It turned out an impeller vane failed in the engine-driven fuel pump causing the rollback. Got it fixed that night, and it performed admirably for the rest of the show.

The demo in the SJ30 was not much to see. With only 5 minutes to use, and with a corporate jet, there's not much you can do; Short field takeoff, fly by fast, fly by slow, short field landing…done.

The really cool part of the show was watching the show from the second floor of the well-catered chalets that lined the demonstration runway. There, on full display, the hottest military and civilian hardware pulling all the stops out to vie for their much-coveted defense and civilian contracts. I have to say that flying in the show was a bit of a letdown, being so quick and uneventful, although it was somewhat disconcerting and not a little distracting to see the latest fire control radars track your every move.

The week went by pretty quickly, and with no further catastrophes, my thoughts turned to the trip home, hoping for a less eventful flight home than had been offered us on the way over. At least with the GPS, reasonable navigation could be assumed.

We left and flew nonstop from Paris to Reykjavik, with both aircraft and equipment performing flawlessly. We had planned to make Bangor before nightfall, so after a quick fuel and weather check, we were on our way. Cleared for takeoff, off we went. V1, Rotate, climb, gear and flaps up, clear left for the on-course vector and… oh shit. The left wing was covered with red hydraulic fluid. Gear back down, flaps full, turn downwind, and land.

OK…. I get that this is a prototype, but COME ON!!

The mechs there in Reykjavik were first-rate, and with just a few phones calls back and forth to San Antonio, a solution was designed, and parts were on the way. It took a few days, but we enjoyed our time in Reykjavik and were confident that the solution would work and that the necessary disassembly/reassembly would go without a hitch. And it did. Sort of…Winging our way to Narsarsuaq, things were looking pretty good…Until….

Here we go again. One hundred miles out of Narsarsuaq, the GPS craps out. We had DME, but it was only accurate inside 15 or so miles, and with the visibility deteriorating, we were relegated to flying a North/South search pattern of sorts over southwestern Greenland in what we thought was the general vicinity of the airport looking for a DME lock that we could use. We lucked out and got a DME lock pretty quickly, and when the DME showed a minimum, we looked down, and lo and behold, there it was. A quick spiral down to land, all the while watching the weather deteriorate. They weren't kidding about the rapidly changing weather here. A quick weather check showed less than optimum weather at our next stop, Goose Bay, Newfoundland. Metro reported clouds at Goose Bay were solid from 400 feet to 10000 feet. Not a big deal, but with the reported light to moderate icing in the cloud and us without any de-ice, it presented us with an interesting challenge. Well, at least they had an ILS, so on we pressed.

On initial contact with Goose Bay Approach control, we informed them that our approach would have to be just a bit unorthodox because we have no deice on board. The plan was to dirty up above the overcast (10000'), wait until we were well above the glide slope, then dive down, attempting to intercept the glide slope from above somewhere around 2000' AGL, thus minimizing our time in the icing conditions.

It sounds like a reasonably good plan and approach control was more than accommodating. Of course, what we weren't expecting was that shortly after entering the clouds, the pitot heat circuit breaker popped, and our airspeed indication went to zero. So…Reset the breaker, airspeed came back up. No wait…I'm sorry…*first*, <u>find</u> the breaker. A mad scramble, then reset it. 15 seconds later, the breaker pops, airspeed zero, reset again…We went through this little dance 5 more times before we broke out. Me, flying attitude and power settings, and Bill reaching across to get to the breaker, thus allowing me a brief peek every 15 seconds or so at our airspeed... It was controlled pandemonium for at least a while on the approach. Fortunately, the "glide slope intercept from above" part worked out uncharacteristically nicely. - We intercepted the glide slope at 1200 feet or so and followed it down till we broke out at 400 feet. Whereupon (wait for it…) the tower matter of factly informed us that the braking condition on the roll-out end of the runway was reported as nil. Nil means zero… as in, you're not stopping. Nil braking action is a big deal when you *do* have reverse thrust available to you. Without it, landing that way is just plain stupid. Fortunately, when we learned that the braking action on the *touchdown* end was good, I made an instant decision to circle to land on the opposite direction runway where at least our rollout would have decent braking. So, around we circled

…at 300 feet in and out of the ragged virga clawing down from the grey clouds, the tower guys gawking at us at what seemed to us to be eye level. Luck smiled on us once again, and we landed successfully, rolling out without any blown tires or damaged egos.

At this point, this constant "problem/solution", "problem/solution" was beginning to wear on us. Bill and I both just wanted to be done.

A quick weather brief portended clear skies shortly after takeoff en route to Bangor, Maine, our last stop on our way home. The icing problem on departure remained an issue, but it would be fun to deal with at least this time. So, we takeoff, level at 200 feet, built up a nice head of steam (250 knots or so), then pitch up 30 degrees and blast through the icing layers and into the golden sunshine at 10000 feet. Nice.

As forecast, the weather was severe and clear just 50 miles south, and the remainder of our flight to Bangor was as relaxing and disaster-free as anyone could hope for.

It looked as if the rest was downhill all the way. Clear skies and light winds allowed a nonstop flight plan to San Antonio, our home sweet home. But alas, Murphy's law wasn't done with us yet.

I had decided that with all we'd been through, and despite Ed's restriction on who was to fly, I was determined to let Bill fly the last leg home. He had certainly earned it. Any guesses on how *that* turned out?

Halfway down the runway on takeoff, the right engine decided it didn't like its turbine section anymore and proceeded to eat it. Bill did the immediate right thing and rejected the takeoff.

We limped back to the gate, more than a little dismayed, but knowing that because this fix would require an engine change, we were at last ready to call it over with and wing our way home commercially. And home we went.

Three weeks later, I flew to Bangor and ferried the plane home to San Antonio—a beautiful flight, nonstop, with clear skies the whole way. A reward, I liked to think, for having persevered through the challenges presented to us earlier.

And maybe that's what it is all about. We learn little about an airplane when things go swimmingly. More importantly, we learn less about *ourselves* when presented with a problem-free life. I think we mistakenly think life is more fun…more rewarding when things go easy. It does seem that way…I'll give you that. It certainly is fun…those times when it all works out. But, to my mind, it is far more rewarding and *fun* when less-than-ideal circumstances are thrown in our way, and we rise to defeat them. The feeling of conquering insurmountable obstacles is a life-affirming feat that makes a life richer and more colorful.

THE GREATEST FLYER OF THEM ALL!

And so, we come to this. The greatest of them all, Numero uno. The exemplar of all things aerodynamic. The undisputed king of the skies with an unprecedented air-to-air combat kill ratio - freakishly maneuverable - uniquely evolved to maintain aerial superiority through the ages and exists today as the envy of all real flyers.

So…

Von Richthofen? Rickenbacker? Hartman? Yeager?

All masters of the air, to be sure, but no. I speak of none other than the mighty Dragonfly - Odonata Anisoptera., A marvel of aerodynamic engineering, 300 million years in the making, selectively evolved to incorporate advanced aerodynamic structure, physiology, and propulsive efficiency into its unbeatable bag of aeronautical awesomeness.

The dragonfly is a tandem wing flying insect. But what makes it unique among the other tandem-winged flyers is its muscle-to-wing control mechanism. You see, with most tandem wing flyers, the four wings attach directly to the abdomen, and control is affected by a single set of muscles to achieve the desired wing action.

This is a fairly limiting mechanism that severely restricts the possible combinations of wing-to-wing interaction. The dragonfly, on the other hand, uses *individual* muscles to control each of its sets of wings. This allows the dragonfly to position its rear wings at different angles to the front, to allow each set of wings to beat in phase or out of phase and enables the varying of each wing's angle of incidence, sweep, dihedral, and twist, all this, mind you, while flapping at 30 beats per second.

Among other things, this unique relationship enables ultra-high-speed fight and almost instantaneous acceleration to 35 plus mph, or 100 body lengths per second! To put that in perspective, a Huey Cobra helicopter would have to fly more than 3000 mph to achieve the same 100 body lengths per second!

But speed alone is not sufficient to lead in the air. Fortunately, this system also allows for super tight nine "G" turns at almost any speed, the ability to fly backward and sideways, straight up and straight down, and of course, hover. And it is this unique wing-to-wing interaction that allows most of this almost magical maneuverability. You no doubt have witnessed their aerial prowess as they seemingly "beam" themselves around the sky—left, right, up and down—in the mere blink of an eye.

The further beauty of this arrangement is in the way the wings interact with *each other* to provide more efficient power production while, at the same time, lowering energy usage. In some modes of flight, the forward wings are purposely positioned to direct airflow over the prepositioned rear wings to enhance the efficiency of lift and drag control and to minimize the energy required. In other modes, the wings twist to produce tiny bound vortices on the wings, effecting a sort of boundary layer control, thus further broadening its already significant maneuvering envelope.

Speaking of drag, because the dragonfly utilizes a forward and up, then down and aft wing motion as opposed to the more common "horizontal stroke", the drag vector produced by the aft/down moving wing actually generates an "up force" to help supplement the dragonfly's "lift".

Paradoxically, whereas drag is seen as the bane of modern aerodynamics, it seems at least one difference enabling much of the dragonfly's speed and maneuvering efficiency.

A still closer look at the dragonfly's wing reveals a subtle but key component to enable it to function efficiently within its sizable operating envelope. The small dark squares, or pterostigmata, on the outboard leading edge of its wings act as an inertial regulator whose purpose is to combat high-speed flutter and enhance aeroelastic behavior. This allows increased flexibility without the attendant stress fractures and in essence allows for higher-speed flight than would otherwise be the case.

OK, so maneuverability is one thing, but it is certainly not all that makes a winning combat vehicle. True. Ask any fighter pilot what is most important in a dogfight, and they will no doubt tell you that spotting their prey and maintaining sight is crucial to winning the engagement. Or, as is said, "lose sight, lose fight."

Once again, the mighty dragonfly stands above the rest. Utilizing its 30,000 optical facets or ommatidia (what we would call lenses), positioned spherically around its significant eyes, the dragonfly builds in his mind a mosaic of overlapping pictures enabling a 360-degree field of view without the petty necessity of turning or tilting its head.

And though they haven't developed any of the stealth features of today's front-line fighters, the dragonfly is not without its own breed of stealth behavior. Researchers have found that when pursuing their prey, the dragonfly purposely "shadows" their moves, maneuvering so precisely and so quickly, matching their prey, move for move, that they appear to the prey to be stationary.

Then, once within striking distance, the dragonfly's forward-mounted six legs grab decisively at their prey without having to alter their bodies' angle of attack (and incurring the attendant drag rise), striking the unsuspecting victim with such colliding force that it renders them fatally stunned and helpless.

It is interesting to note that the dragonfly's air combat technique is not like some modern-day, tried and true fighter tactics. Eric "Bubi" Hartman, arguably the world's greatest air combat fighter, talked openly about his technique:

"I see the enemy first, then close secretly from behind, strike and breakaway to set up the next kill". Any of this sound familiar?

Sadly, however, all this magnificence comes at a cost. Although the larval and nymph stages of early dragonfly development can last up to two years, the emerging fully developed adult has an average life span of only 2 to 4 *weeks*. Not surprisingly, adult dragonflies spend the majority of their waking hours eating or mating. Not the worst way to spend your life…

Still, 4 weeks is just too short for these extraordinary creatures..

So, the next time you're out for a walk by the lake, stop for just a moment and take the time to marvel at these gossamer-winged, iridescent beauties. They are unquestionably one of life's truly magnificent creations.

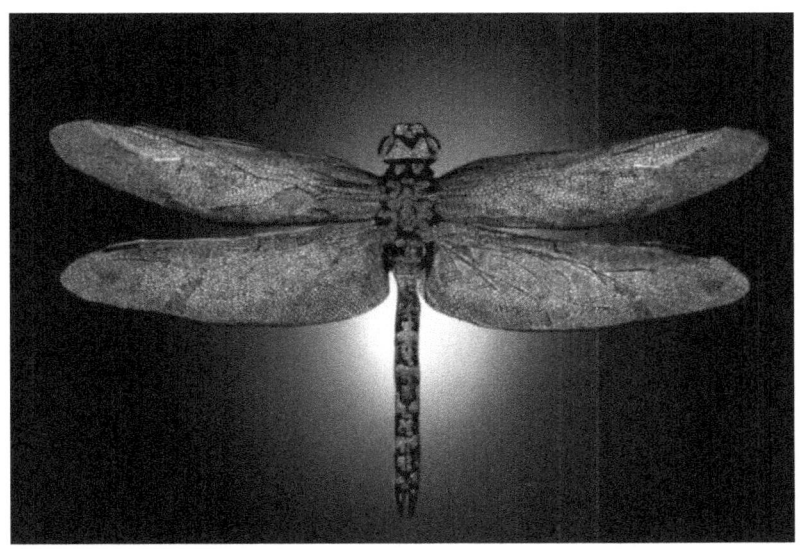

GLOSSARY

Angels

Altitude, in thousands of feet (ie Angels 10 = 10,000 feet)

AOA

Angle of Attack

ATIS

Automatic Terminal Information Service

BN

Bombardier / Navigator (Right Seater in the A6 Intruder)

Bolter

Touchdown on flight deck but failure to grab a wire

Cat

Short for Catapult

Cherubs

Altitude in Hundreds of feet, (ie Cherubs 4 = 400 feet)

Clag

Crappy, Cloudy, Rainy/ Yucky Weather Conditions

Drogue

The hose that extends from the Tankers Store to allow refueling

FOD

Foreign Object Debris or Foreign Object Damage

"G" Suit

A bladder filled corset, fitted around legs and stomach that inflates with air to forestall blood draining to the lower extremities during high "G" maneuvers

HUD

Heads Up Display

GLOSSARY

ILS
　Instrument Landing System - Displays Glideslope and azimuth (Localizer) information

IMC
　Instrument Meteorological Conditions

LOC
　Localizer

Marshall Instructions
　Holding Pattern instructions

Marshaler
　A person who directs aircraft on the flight deck (ie a Yellow Shirt)

N1/N2
　A measure of the Rotational Speed of the LOW/HIGH Pressure Compressor /Turbine in a jet engine

RadAlt
　Radar Altimeter

RAT
　Ram air turbine

Ramp
　The very aftmost part of a Aircraft Carrier's flight deck

RIO
　Radar Intercept Officer (the back seater, a Naval Flight Officer, in the F4 and F14)

Rudder Shaker
　A method by which the rudder pedals of an aircraft are mechanically vibrated to warn of an impending aerodynamic stall

GLOSSARY

SID

Standard Instrument Departure

Signal Buster

Expedite your return to the Carrier

Sim

Simulator

Tacan

"Tactical Air Navigation" A navigational aid providing both Azimuth and Distance (DME) information to a particular location

Texaco

Shipboard call sign for Tanker Aircraft

TOP

Turbine Outlet Pressure - a factor when determining a turbine engine's power output

Trap

An arrested landing

VMC

Visual Meteorological Conditions

ZULU

Greenwich Mean Time

ABOUT THE AUTHOR

Carl Pascarell's aviation experience extends to virtually all areas of high performance aviation. He began flying as a teenager and since has amassed nearly 44,000 hours in more than 420 different types of aircraft.

After graduating from Rensselaer Polytechnic Institute with a degree in Aeronautical Engineering, Carl entered Navy Flight Training. He received his "Wings of Gold" in October of 1976. He completed two Mediterranean cruises flying the Vought Corsair II aboard the USS Independence and the USS Eisenhower. He was subsequently assigned to VT-4 in Pensacola, Florida, as an advanced jet instructor flying the TA4 Skyhawk. Military Commendations include the Navy Air Medal with Bronze Star, The Navy Commendation Award, The Navy Achievement Award, and The Vought Flight Achievement Award.

He is a degreed Aeronautical Engineer, Ex-Navy Carrier Pilot, Experimental Test Pilot, Air Show Pilot and published aviation author. He holds a surface level aerobatic waiver in several aircraft and has been a designated Aerobatic Competency Evaluator (ACE) since the program's inception.

Carl was a founding member of the Redhawks Precision Formation Aerobatic Team and along with teammates Harry Shepard and Bob Gandt flew for 11 years the exotic SF-260 Marchetti in one of the few "military style" formation aerobatic performances ever presented on the airshow circuit.

In his capacity as Chief Test Pilot for Swearingen Aircraft, he has twice performed at the prestigious Paris Airshow in two different experimental prototype turbine powered aircraft.

Carl has been instructing in the Pitts S2 and Extra 300 at the St. Augustine Airport for nearly 25 years, training pilots of all ages, experience levels, and aspirations. He is a respected authority on aerobatics and formation flying and prides himself on turning out competent, knowledgeable and safe aerobatic pilots.

www.ingramcontent.com/pod-product-compliance
Lightning Source LLC
Chambersburg PA
CBHW061604110426
42742CB00039B/2769